D1710499

ART AND COINAGE
IN MAGNA GRAECIA

ART AN

IN MAG

R. ROSS HOLLOWAY

D COINAGE
NA GRAECIA

EDIZIONI ARTE E MONETA, PUBLISHERS · BELLINZONA

Distributed in North America by
Abner Schram (Schram Enterprises Ltd.)
36 Park St.
Montclair, N.J. 07042
ISBN 0-8390-0206-8

Uxori Delectissimae
Dulces Concorditer Agimus Annos

The following pages are intended to illustrate and discuss the coinage of Greek South Italy of the fifth and fourth centuries B.C. as part of the history of Greek art. They rely on the patient work of numismatic research which has been carried on since Prospero Parisi treated the coins of Magna Graecia in the sixteenth century and on the reflections of archaeologists accumulated since the time when Winckelmann discovered the genius of Greek art in the coins of Syracuse. However, in writing for a circle of readers beyond numismatists and archaeologists, it is not my intention to disguise the incomplete state of the study of these coinages, which makes it impossible to compose a connected history of western Greek coin art in the full sense of the word and which is clearly reflected in the contradictory opinions as to the chronology of single issues expressed by the most eminent contemporary authorities. The result is a series of essays and notes, connected by common themes and by these coins, that are fully worthy of inspection and reflection.

This book owes its existence to the initiative of the directors of the Edizioni Arte e Moneta, and it is a pleasant duty to thank them for their stimulation and their constant efforts to further my work. Photographic permissions were courteously extended by the institutions and officials concerned. I have pursued the composition of these pages with the outstanding facilities of the American Numismatic Society and the Brown University Library, as well as with companions in research and travels of the Catholic University of Louvain.

DESCRIPTIVE INDEX OF COINS DISCUSSED

Unless otherwise identified the coins illustrated are from private collections.   Abbreviations are listed on p. 167.

TARENTUM

I

obverse: Hero, seated r. holding distaff and kantharos. ΤΑΡΑΣ (Tarentum).
reverse: Hero, riding dolphin r., below, cockle-shell. ΤΑΡΑΣ.
Silver,   8.05 gr. Stater, ca. 480 B.C. (Cahn). Naples, National Archaeological Museum.

2

obverse: Hero riding dolphin l., below, cockle-shell. ΤΑΡΑΣ.
reverse: Male head l. within circle.
Silver,   7.88 gr. Stater, 480-470 B.C. (Cahn).

3

obverse: Hero riding dolphin r., below, cockle-shell. ΤΑΡΑΣ.
reverse: Head r., within an olive wreath.
Silver,   8.19 gr. Stater, ca. 470-460 B.C. (Cahn).

4

obverse: Hero riding dolphin r. over waves. ΤΑΡΑΣ.
reverse: Horseman r.
Silver,   7.80 gr.   Stater, ca. 450–430 B.C. (Evans Period I).

5

obverse: Armed rider vaulting from horse l.
reverse: Armed hero riding dolphin l. ΤΑΡΑΣ.
Silver,   7.82 gr.   Stater, ca. 420–380 B.C. (Evans Period II).

6

obverse: Horseman r. ΘΡΑ.
reverse: Hero with trident riding dolphin r. ΤΑΡΑΣ.
Silver,   7.90 gr.   Stater, ca. 380–345 B.C. (Evans Period III).

7

obverse: Nude male figure bridling horse mounted by boy jockey.
        ΚΑΛ, Δ.
reverse: Hero with bow and arrows riding dolphin r. ΤΑΡΑΣ. Φ Ι.
Silver,   7.84 gr.   Stater, ca. 344–334 B.C. (Evans Period IV).

8

obverse: Head of Hera, r. veiled.
reverse: Poseidon seated l., supplicated by child l., in field, a star and Ͱ
        below, stool. Κ. ΤΑΡΑΝΤΙΝΩΝ (Of the Tarentines).
Gold,   8.56 gr. Stater, ca. 344–334 B.C. (Evans Period IV). Berlin,
        Staatliche Museen.

9

obverse: Horseman with spear r., in field symbol (?), below, Φ.
reverse: Hero with spindle riding dolphin l. over waves, in field, an eagle.
Silver,   7.92 gr.   Stater, ca. 334-330 B.C. (Evans Period V).

10

obverse: Head of Zeus r.
reverse: Thunderbolt. To l. lance. ΑΛΕΞΑΝΔΡΟΥ ΤΟΥ ΝΕΟΠΤΟΛΕΜΟΥ. (Alexander the Son of Neoptolemos).
Gold,   8.57 gr.   Stater, ca. 334-330 B.C. (Evans Period V). London, British Museum.

11

obverse: Victory leading armed horseman l.
reverse: Hero with spear and shield vaulting from dolphin l. ΤΑΡΑΣ, Ι ΟΡ, on shield Ε.
Silver,   7.98 gr.   Stater, ca. 302-281 B.C. (Evans Period VI).

RHEGIUM

I

obverse: Lion's head facing.
reverse: Calf's head l. ΡΕΓΙΝΟΝ. (Of the Rhegians).
Silver,   17,22 gr.   Tetradrachm, 488-480 B.C. (see p. 41).

2

obverse: Biga of mules r.; in exergue a laurel leaf.
reverse: Hare r. ΡΕΓΙΝΟΝ.
Silver,   17.37 gr. Tetradrachm, 480-461 B.C.   (Franke and Kraay).

3

obverse: Lion's head seen from above.
reverse: A hero or divinity seated within a laurel wreath l.   ΡΕΓΙΝΟΣ.
(Of the city of Rhegium).
Silver,   17.19 gr. Tetradrachm, Herzfelder no. 31a, 445-435 B.C.

4

obverse: similar.
reverse: similar.
Silver,   17.28 gr. Tetradrachm, Herzfelder no. 52, 435-425 B.C.

5

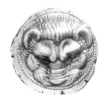 

obverse: Lion's head seen from above.
reverse: Head of Apollo r., crowned with laurel. Behind, an olive sprig.
ΡΕΓΙΝΟΝ.
Silver,   17.18 gr. Tetradrachm, Herzfelder no. 77, 415/410-387 B.C.

6

obverse: Head of Apollo l., crowned with laurel.
reverse: Lion's head seen from above.
Silver,   15.83 gr. Tetradrachm, Herzfelder no. 115, ca. 356-351 B.C.

POSEIDONIA

I

obverse: Poseidon brandishing trident r. ΠΟΜΕΙ. (Poseidonia).
reverse: Bull walking l. ΠΟΜΕ. (Poseidonia).
Silver,   8.09 gr. Stater, 440-420 B.C. (Kraay)[1].

2

obverse: similar. Behind, an incense burner.
reverse: Bull standing r. ΠΟΣΕΙΔΩΝΙΑ (Poseidonia), below, ΔΟΣΣΕΝΝΟ (Dossennos).
Silver,   7.64 gr. Stater, 350-325 B.C. (Kraay and Zancani)[2].

CAULONIA

I

obverse: Apollo moving r., spirit (daimon) on outstretched l. arm. In field l. a bovine skull (bucranium) within a wreath. To r. a stag on a pedestal.
reverse: A stag r. ΚΑΥΛΟΝΙΑΤΑΜ (Of Caulonia).
Silver,   8.08 gr. Stater, 435-425 B.C. (Kraay)[3].

METAPONTUM

1

obverse: Ear of grain, cricket. META (Metapontum).
reverse: River god (Acheloos) standing and holding libation bowl (patera) and reed stalk. ΑΕΘΛΟΝ ΑΨΕΛΟΙΟ (The prize of Acheloos).
Silver, 7.63 gr. Stater, ca. 490-470 B.C. (Franke), ca. 450 B.C. (Kraay), Noe no. 311.

2

obverse: Ear of grain. META.
reverse: Apollo standing and holding laurel sapling and bow.
Silver, 8.03 gr. Stater, ca. 485-475 B.C. (Franke), ca. 450 B.C. (Kraay), ca. 465-440 B.C. (Robinson), Noe no. 314.

3

obverse: Ear of grain. META.
reverse: Heracles standing with bow and club.
Silver, 7.93 gr. Stater, ca. 485-470 B.C. (Franke), ca. 450 B.C. (Kraay), ca. 465-440 B.C. (Robinson), Noe no. 313.

4

obverse: Apollo seated with lyre, in field, laurel sapling r.
reverse: Ear of grain, cricket. META.
Silver, 7.68 gr. Stater, later fifth century, Noe no. 431.

5

obverse: Head of Dionysos three-quarter l. **ΚΑΛ.**
reverse: Ear of grain, snake. **ΜΕΤΑ** and **ΦΙΛΟ.**
Silver,   7.99 gr. Stater, ca. 435–350 B.C. (Robinson).

6

obverse: Head of divinity with ram's horn r.
reverse: Ear of grain. **ΜΕΤΑ.**
Silver,   7.48 gr. Stater, ca. 435–350 B.C. (Robinson), ca. 435–410
(Kraay)[4], Noe no. 344.

7

obverse: Head of Persephone r.
reverse: Grain ear, plow. **ΜΕΤΑ** and **ΜΑ.**
Silver,   7.93 gr. Stater, ca. 330–300 B.C. (Kraay and Franke).

8

obverse: Head of Victory r. **ΝΙΚΑ** (Victory).
reverse: Ear of grain and pomegranate. **ΜΕΤΑΠΟΝΤΙΟΝ.** (Of the Metapontines).
Silver,   7.79 gr. Stater, ca. 400–360 B.C. (Naster), Noe no. 495.

9

obverse: Bearded head helmeted r. On helmet bowl, a four-horse chariot
driven by Victory. Below the bowl on the neckguard, a winged
hippocamp. In the field, forepart of a horse and **ΑΠΗ.**
reverse: Ear of grain. A club and **ΑΜΙ. ΜΕΤΑΠΟΝΤΙΝΩΝ.**
Silver,   15.88 gr. Distater, ca. 330–300 B.C. (Kraay and Franke).

10

obverse: Head of Demeter, r., veiled.
reverse: Ear of grain. METAΠONT.
Silver, 7.48 gr. Stater, 344-334 B.C. (see p. 71).

THURII

1

obverse: Head of Athene r.
reverse: Walking bull r. ΘOYPIΩN (Of the Thurians).
Silver, 7.95 gr. Stater, ca. 443-415/410 B.C. (Franke), ca. 420 B.C.
(Jenkins), ca. 415-400 B.C. (Kraay).

2

obverse: Head of Athene r.
reverse: Butting bull r., in exergue, panther. ΘOYPIΩN and ΣΩ.
Silver, 7.95 gr. Stater, ca. 415/410-400 B.C. (Franke), ca. 375 B.C.
(Kraay).

HERACLEA

I

obverse: Head of Athene superimposed on aegis r.
reverse: Heracles seated on lion's skin, holding cup, club beside him. ΗΕΡΑΚΛΕΙΩΝ (Of the Herakleians).
Silver,   7.92 gr. Stater, 432 B.C. (Robinson), Work no. 7.

2

obverse: Head of Athene facing.
reverse: Heracles wrestling lion. ΗΡΑΚΛΕΩΝ.
Silver,   7.58 gr. Stater, 410-400 B.C. (Jenkins), Work no. 23.

3

obverse: Head of Athene r. ΑΘΑΝΑΕ (Athene).
reverse: Heracles wrestling lion. In field, club and bow. ΗΡΑΚΛΕΩΝ.
Silver,   7.85 gr. Stater, ca. 433/432-400 B.C. (Franke), ca. 350-330 B.C. (Kraay), Work no. 25.

4

obverse: Head of Athene r.
reverse: Heracles wrestling lion. Below EY. In exergue, a stalk of grain. ΗΕΡΑΚΕΙΩΝ.
Silver,   7.73 gr. Stater, ca. 433/432-400 B.C. (Franke), soon after 400 B.C. (Robinson), ca. 375 B.C. (Kraay), Work no. 8.

5

obverse: Head of Athene r., behind Ⱶ Η. ΗΡΑΚΛΕΙΩΝ.
reverse: Heracles standing with lion's skin and club, holding cup in extended hand. An altar. In field, a thunderbolt.
Silver, 6.10 gr. Stater, soon after 280 B.C. (Robinson).

CROTON

1

obverse: Heracles seated l. on lion's skin holding branch. Beside him a bow, before him an altar on which a sacrifice is burning. To r. ΟΙΚΙΣΤΑΣ (founder).
reverse: Tripod, barley grain and Ε. ΚΡΟ (Kroton).
Silver, 7.59 gr. Stater, ca. 420-390 B.C. (Franke), ca 420 B.C. (Kraay), ca. 400 B.C. (Jenkins).

2

obverse: similar.
reverse: Tripod, Apollo drawing bow against Python. ΚΡΟΤΟΝ.
Silver, 7.65 gr. Stater, date as no. 1.

3

obverse: Head of Hera facing, B.
reverse: Heracles seated on lion's skin l. holding cup, his club beside him. ΚΡΟΤΩΝΙΑΤΑΣ (Of Croton).
Silver, 7.75 gr. Stater, ca. 410-380 B.C. (Franke), ca. 360 B.C. (Kraay), 400-350 B.C. (Robinson).

4

obverse: Head of Apollo r. **ΚΡΟΤΩΝΙΑΤΑΣ**.
reverse: The infant Heracles strangling snakes.
Silver, 7.83 gr. Stater, ca. 390-387/380 B.C. (Franke), ca. 350 B.C. (Kraay), ca. 340 B.C. (Jenkins), 400-350 B.C. (Robinson).

PANDOSIA

1

obverse: Head of Hera facing.
reverse: Pan seated l. holding two spears, before him a herm, beside him a dog. ΠΑΝΔΟΣΙΝ (Pandosia).
Silver, 7.10 gr. Stater, ca. 400 B.C. (Head). New York, American Numismatic Society.

2

obverse: similar.
reverse: Pan seated l., dog to l.
Bronze, 2,09 gr. Unit, ca. 400 B.C. (Head). Naples, National Archaeological Museum.

1

obverse: Head of Nymph within olive wreath r. ΤΕΡΕΙ (Terina).
reverse: Victory.
Silver, 7.93 gr. Stater, 480-450 B.C. (Unknown to Regling).

2

obverse: Head of Nymph within olive wreath l.
reverse: Victory seated on water jar (hydria) l.
Silver, 7.69 gr. Stater, 445-425 B.C. (Regling no. 9).

3

obverse: Head of Nymph within olive wreath r. Behind Φ.
reverse: Victory seated l. before fountain. On Victory's seat A H.
ΤΕΡΙΝΑ (Terina).
Silver, 7.43 gr. Stater, 425-420 B.C. (Regling no. 34).

4

obverse: Head of Nymph r.
reverse: Victory leaning on columnar support. A bird perched on a base.
Silver, 7.60 gr. Stater, 420-400 B.C. (Regling no. 37).

5

obverse: Head of Nymph r. ΤΕΡΙΝΑΙΟΝ (Of the Terinians).
reverse: Victory seated l.
Silver,   7.78 gr. Stater, 425-420 B.C. (Regling no. 43).

6

obverse: Head of Nymph r. Behind Γ. ΤΕΡΙΝΑΙΟΝ.
reverse: Victory seated l. On base Π. In field a monogram?
Silver,   8.01 gr. Stater, 420-400 B.C. (Regling no. 43-41).

7

obverse: Head of Nymph r. Behind Π (not visible in this specimen).
          ΤΕΡΙΝΑΙΟΝ.
reverse: Victory seated l.
Silver,   7.75 gr. Stater, 420-400 B.C. (Regling no. 64).

8

obverse: Head of Nymph r. ΤΕΡΙΝΑΙΩΝ.
reverse: Victory seated l.
Silver,   7.65 gr. Stater, after 400 B.C. (Regling no. 78). New York,
American Numismatic Society.

VELIA

1

obverse: Forepart of lion devouring prey r.
reverse: Incuse.
Silver,   3.90 gr. Drachm, 530-490 B.C. (Breglia)⁵.

2

obverse: Female head r.
reverse: Lion r., above owl. [ΥΕ]ΛΗΤΕΩΝ (Of the Velians).
Silver,   7.60 gr. Stater, before 450 B.C. (Head).

3

obverse: Head of Athene l.
reverse: Lion attacking deer l. ΥΕΛΗΤΩΝ.
Silver,   7.53 gr. Stater, ca. 420 (Robinson), ca. 380 B.C. (Jenkins)⁶.

4

obverse: Head of Athene facing, on visor ΚΛΕΥΔΟΡΟΥ (artist's signature).
reverse: Ravening lion l. ΥΕΛΗΤΩΝ.
Silver,   7.66 gr. Stater, ca. 380-340 B.C. (Franke), ca. 350 B.C. (Kraay).

obverse: Head of Athene r., on crest of helmet ΦΙΛΙΣΤΙΩΝ (artists' signature).

reverse: Glowering lion l., sword or spearhead in mouth, at edge of sea, above Victory, ΥΕΛΗΤΩΝ and Φ.

Silver, 7.52 gr. Stater, begins about 320 B.C. (Robinson).

NOTES TO THE DESCRIPTIVE INDEX OF COINS DISCUSSED.

[1] C. M. KRAAY, 'Gli stateri a doppio rilievo di Poseidonia', *Atti e Memorie della Società Magna Grecia*, n.s. vol. 8, 1967, pp. 113-135.

[2] KRAAY as cited, see also P. ZANCANI-MONTUORO, 'Dossenno a Poseidonia', *Atti e Memorie della Società Magna Grecia*, n.s. vol. 2, 1958, pp. 79-94.

[3] C. M. KRAAY, 'Caulonia and South Italian Problems', *NC*, series 6, vol. 20, 1960, pp. 53-82. S. P. NOE, *The Coinage of Caulonia*, Numismatic Studies no. 9, New York, 1958, Group G.

[4] C. M. KRAAY, 'Two Late Fifth Century Hoards from South Italy', *Schweizerische Numismatische Rundschau*, vol. 49, 1970, p. 53.

[5] L. BREGLIA, 'Notizie sulla monetazione arcaica di Velia', *La Parola del Passato*, vol. 108-110, 1966, pp. 227-240.

[6] The dates of this and the following two coins would be lowered to the period 320-287 B. C. following L. BRUNETTI, 'Contributo alla cronologia delle zecche di Velia e Neapolis', *Rivista Italina di Numismatica e Scienze Affini*, vol. 57, 1955, pp. 5-34.

In the eyes of their contemporaries, the Greeks of South Italy inhabited a vast new wold. 'Greece on a grand scale' was what they felt when they called Italian Greece 'He Megale Hellas' or, as we know the phrase better today in its Latin form, 'Magna Graecia'. If understood only in a geographical sense there is a strange inexactness in this name. South Italy is smaller than Asia Minor, the coasts of which were Greek since the Bronze Age, and the vastness of the Balkan heartland and the steppes of Russia behind the Greek colonies around the Black Sea coasts far outran comparison with the plains of Apulia or the southern Apennines. But as an impression of scale, of the achievement of the Greek cities on the Italian coasts, the name is a powerful reminder of the stature of this segment of Hellenism. Little remains of these Greek cities, even in comparison with the remains of Greek Sicily. Their literature is almost entirely lost, and their history is reduced to an occasional fragment of information. But their coins survive. Among them are masterpieces of coin art, and more than a few types with an element of originality in design that invites speculation over the circumstances surrounding their creation. This volume is a presentation of the coins of Magna Graecia as they figure in the history of Greek art. But it is necessarily more than that, since the history of art is the history of culture. And these same coins embody the spirit that made Magna Graecia a distinguishable and individual element in the greater whole of Greek culture.

The cultural unity of Magna Graecia is hardly apparent from the tatters of its political and military history. The history of the region begins, for all practical purposes, with the destruction of Siris and Sybaris by their sister-cities in the sixth century B.C., and these events set the tone for much of what followed. Yet the same cities participated for the most part in the national league which was created in the sixth century and revived at the end of the fifth century under the influence of Croton. Proof of their sense of identity is given by the early coins of the area, belonging to the later sixth and early fifth centuries B.C., which have been presented in the series of 'Edizioni Arte e Moneta' by Giovanni Gorini[1]. These are the distinctive incuse issues, which repeat the obverse type intaglio on the reverse and share a paper-thin fabric, a weight standard, and the decorative borders of the dies.

The coinage of the two centuries and more beginning in the early fifth century, which it is our task to illustrate here, is subject to the intrusion of influence from abroad and differences in the individual series brought on by their own internal growth. Yet regional homogeneity is not fully broken down. Types are shared between mints, for example, the facing head obverses of Croton and Pandosia. And, in general, the coinages of Magna Graecia in this period of high classical Greek art show a desire to bring physical animation to the subjects of their coin types, together with a desire to transfer discoveries

[1] *La Monetazione incusa della Magna Grecia*, Milan, 1975.

in the representation of pictorial space to coin art. These aesthetic tendencies common to the region perpetuate a common spirit in its coinage.

At the opening of the fifth century B.C. the Greek cities of South Italy counted two centuries or more of history. The nucleus of their populations were Greeks from the north central Peloponnesos (Achaia). Spartans, however, had founded Tarentum, the Locrians from north of the Gulf of Corinth had their colony of Locri Epizephyrii, settlers from the island of Euboia beside Attica and Boeotia established Rhegium. Moreover, there had been a cosmopolitan element in the colonies from the beginning, when Greeks from Asia Minor took part in the foundation of Siris, and later, in 530, when Velia was settled by people of the city of Phocaia (also in Asia Minor) fleeing Persian domination and expelled by Carthage from their foothold in Corsica.

Achaian Sybaris grew wealthy and luxurious from its role of commercial intermediary between Asia Minor and Italy. But shortly before 500 B.C. Sybaris fell before an alliance led by its neighbor Croton, and in the years immediately thereafter Croton stood at the apex of its power. Nothing could diminish the attraction of the plain of Sybaris, small in area, and closed in by the first hills of the Calabrian mountains but commanding access through the valley of the Cratis to the interior and thence to the Tyrrhenian coast where Sybaris had established her own colonies at Laos, Pyxus, and Poseidonia. These cities served as portage stations for Sybarite commerce (clearly luxury goods small in bulk but great in value) destined for the north and especially Etruria, permitting the Sybarites to avoid shipping through the Straits of Messina which could be closed by Rhegium and Messina. For more than fifty years the village that remained on the site of the once-proud Sybaris eked out a precarious existence under the eye of Croton. Then, in 446, the Athenians took advantage of the old Sybarites' claim to promote the establishment of a new city, Thurii, which, in spite of the initial hostility of Croton, succeeded, largely due to the generalship of the Spartan mercenary captain Cleandros.

Croton, a city famous for its doctors and athletes, is set high on a wide promontory divided from the mass of the mountains to the west by its own plain. At the point of the promontory was the renowned Temple of Hera Lacinia and its grove of pine where the flocks of the goddess pastured and gold columns showed the richness of the sanctuary. The Sila range behind Croton is the most impenetrable part of the Calabrian mountains, but, nothing daunted, the Crotonians founded Terina on the Tyrrhenian coast and probably Pandosia in the valley of the Cratis, both of which were to strike elegant coinages beginning in the fifth century. Having won command of the plain of Sybaris and its connections across the mountains, Croton attempted to dominate Locri Epizephyrii, situated to the south where the mountains rise abruptly from the shore and the city was built over three hills, their intervening valleys and the shore. Croton, no doubt, dominated its daughter colony Caulonia north of Locri. But Locri also had her colonies on the Tyrrhenian coast and Syracusan support, which blocked Croton's attempted monopoly of trans-peninsula communications.

The role of Syracuse in the affairs of the western Mediterranean was paramount in the early fifth century. United with Acragas (Agrigentum) she defeated the Carthaginian invasion of Sicily in 480 at Himera and in 474 turned back once and for all the threat of Etruscan encroachment on South Italy at the battle of Cumae fought in waters off the earliest Greek colony in the west, just north of Naples. Although halted at Locri, the Crotonians had secured the transit of the peninsula at just the moment when the two guardians of the Strait of Messina, Rhegium and Messina, fell under the control of one man, Anaxilas the tyrant of Rhegium. When examining the coins of Rhegium we shall have reason to take up Anaxilas' intrigue with a band of Greek fugitives from the island of Samos just off the Turkish coast, who came west fleeing the collapse of the Ionian Greek revolt against their overlord the King of Persia and through whom Anaxilas seized Messina. Anaxilas also commemorated the victory of his mule team at the Olympic games by an appropriate coin type, possibly not the first such commemorative issue, but an early example of individual self-glorification in coinage. The coinage is fanciful as well as bold. The reverse type suggests that the mules ran like hares (illustrated on p. 110)[2]! The tyrant, who gained control of Rhegium in 494, died in 476 and the government of his sons was replaced by a democracy in 461.

In the face of Crotonian hostility Rhegium kept a policy of alliance with Tarentum, placed as it were to menace the flank of Croton's domains. Tarentum, like Syracuse, grew from an island commanding a splendid natural harbor. Unlike the Syracusan metropolis, Tarentum was not successful in conquering the inland states of non-Greek people. Together with triumphs commemorated in sculptural groups dedicated at the national sanctuaries of the Greek homeland, Olympia and Delphi, we hear of at least one major Tarentine defeat, in 473, and the Tarentines' Messapian neighbors caused her trouble for another two centuries. Meanwhile, the Tarentines appear to have assumed a dominant influence over Metapontum, the Greek city situated between the Bradanus and Casuentus Rivers on a featureless but agriculturally rich plain which extends inland along the two river valleys toward modern Matera.

Shortly after 450 B.C. two new cities were founded as successors of the two ill-fated metropolises

[2] The connection of this coin with Anaxilas' victory goes back to Aristotle, cited in the lexicon of Pollux 5.75. According to the same entry, Aristotle explained the type, which also occurs at Messina, as a record of Anaxilas' introducing the hare into Sicily. One may suspect that the great philosopher was guessing — as he did on other occasions, specifically in regard to Solon's 'monetary' reform, *Ath. Pol.* 10 — and furthermore that he was rather insensitive to early fifth century artistic language.

of the sixth century, Sybaris and Siris. The first was Thurii, founded on the old site of Sybaris in 446 by the Athenians as a panhellenic venture. The second was Heraclea, established by the Tarentines near the mouth of the Acris, on the coast just beyond Metapontum and not far from the site formerly occupied by Siris. We know more about the beginning of Thurii than Heraclea; the city-planner Hippodamos is associated with its layout and Herodotus was among the early residents. Physically we know both due to recent excavations which have revealed their checkerboard street plans, an arrangement that had been typical of colonial Greek cities since the seventh century. The site of Heraclea (modern Polichoro) is much like Metapontum, but it controlled by far the easiest, though not the shortest route to the Tyrrhenian coast, an element that must have contributed to Siris' early prosperity and the jealousy of her neighbors, especially Sybaris.

The foundation of Heraclea marks the ascendency of Tarentum in South-Italian affairs. The new city became the seat of a new Italiote-Greek league, from which only Locri, increasingly tied to Syracuse, abstained. However, the friction which was unavoidably generated by the creation of Thurii and Heraclea, and which led to warfare between them, was calmed by the recognition of a new threat menacing the Greek cities from the north. Although the Etruscans had been turned back at Cumae in 474, other groups from the center of the peninsula continued to press south. Cumae and her daughter-city Neapolis survived as Greek cities. But during the later fifth century the rest of Campania was occupied by Italic speakers who had descended along the valleys from the north. Many of the newcomers, whom later history knows as the Campanians, Lucanians and Brettians (from the names of the regions they came to dominate), were often content to merge with the Greek citizens. Naples accepted a significant Oscan-speaking element in her population, and to the south beyond the Sorrento peninsula Poseidonia, visited today because of its three Greek temples, was transformed into a city dominated by the Italic element.

As they moved southward, or as new waves of the northerners came (pressed south by the Gallic invaders who were now seen in northern Italy and who reached and briefly occupied Rome in 394), the Oscans were less easily assimilated. The major preoccupation of the Greek league became defense against this threat. Magna Graecia was largely untouched by the extension of Athenian imperialism into the western Mediterranean beginning in the 440's and culminating in the disastrous defeat before Syracuse in 411. But the Italic threat was augmented as the fourth century opened when the new tyrant of Syracuse, Dionysios I, victorious over a renewed Carthaginian invasion of Sicily (though at frightful cost to the Sicilian Greek cities) sought to extend his power in the peninsula and allied himself with the Lucanians. A number of Greek cities suffered in these years. Caulonia was destroyed (396) and Rhegium sacked (386). Thurii and her neighbors were hard pressed at times, but the Tarentines were led by the statesman, philosopher and soldier Archytas and the situation stabilized. On Archytas' death, however, the Tarentines and their allies began to rely on generals hired from abroad. Archidamas, king of Sparta, was the first. Then in the 330's came Alexander the Molossian, uncle of Alexander the Great. Both died in Italy, with no permanent success despite the momentary luster of Alexander's campaigns that reached all the way to Poseidonia. Cleomenes of Sparta, who came at the turn of the century, was followed in the 270's by Pyrrhus of Epirus in the greatest expedition to have been mounted from Greece in support of the Italiote cities. Pyrrhus' antagonists, however, were not the Lucanians or Brettians, but the Romans, who in the fourth century had consolidated an empire in central Italy including the mountains from which the Oscan speakers had moved south. In 272 the Romans conquered Tarentum, and although Tarentum remained nominally independent and struck coins until the War with Hannibal at the end of the century, her fate and that of the Greek cities of South Italy had been sealed.

The incuse issues of the South Italian Greek cities at the end of the sixth century are excellent examples of some of the greatest strengths of archaic Greek art. They share a simplicity of major design with an ornamental elaboration which produces a sense of the permanent symbol supported by the delicacy of miniature decoration. The same devices were exploited by jewelers (the creators of the so-called Rhodian plaques of the seventh century, for example), and metal-smiths (some of whose finest work, though lost, is mirrored on Athenian black-figured pottery of the same period, typified by the shields of Ajax and Achilles on the well-known vase by Exekias in the Vatican Museum). The art of the gem cutter, it is interesting to observe, is farther removed from these coins than other crafts. Even though Greek (and naturally Etruscan) gems have cable ornament on their borders, the images of the best archaic gem designs convey a sense of movement and action which is not achieved, and perhaps consciously avoided, by the South Italian coins. The figure (Apollo-Hyacinthus) of the incuse series of Tarentum becomes a kind of impatient but confined runner (illustrated on p. 75). Perhaps this is the penalty of composition within a circle (painters of the interior tondos of kylikes sometimes utilized the same running figure type, with similar results); but it may well have been a desirable effect from the point of view of the artist. The types of Poseidonia and Caulonia, both striding divinities seen in profile, are similarly hemmed in by the cable border of the coin, and lose their kinetic force (illustrated on pp. 75-76). Where possible, the type was contrived to impede any possible sense of movement. So the Sybarite bull turns to look backward over its shoulder (illustrated on p. 77), a mannerism repeated by the man-headed bull at Laos[3].

---

[3] This is not the view of J. BAYET, 'Idéologie et plastique I: L'expression des énergies divines dans le monnayage des Grecs', *Mélanges d'archéologie et d'histoire*, vol. 71, 1959, pp. 65-106.

The symbolic value of incuse types (surely the badges of the cities they represent as proposed by Gorini)[4] is shown by their continued life in later phases of the coinages: the tripod of Croton, the grain ear of Metapontum, the Poseidon of Poseidonia, the Apollo of Caulonia, the bull on the small coinages of the independent post-destruction city of Sybaris and as adopted by its successor Thurii (illustrated on p. 128). The later coinages of Magna Graecia would lose much of their interest, however, had they not responded to the movements of Greek art which single out the fifth and fourth centuries B.C. as a culminating moment and which widened the resources at the disposal of the adventurous coin designer.

At the beginning of the fifth century Greek art was passing from its archaic phase (illustrated on p. 78) to the style of simplicity (conventionally known by the German title 'der strenge Stil', 'the Severe Style') characterized by the sculpture of the Temple of Zeus at Olympia (illustrated on p. 79). The flowering of Phidian classicism in Athens after 450 is contemporary with the foundation of Thurii and Heraclea, while the end of the same century introduced the florid style of drapery and composition which in another context I have called post-Phidian expressionism (illustrated on pp. 80-81)[5]. Although responsible for important developments in the representation of emotion and other psychological states, the art of the fourth century was largely concerned with exploiting the discoveries of the fifth and, in many instances, in perpetuating fifth-century types and styles.

Technical factors, as well as taste, were at work in this evolution. To a large extent the much admired simplicity of 'the Severe Style' came about because of the introduction of large-scale hollow-cast bronze sculpture at the end of the sixth century. Faced with the problem of conducting the molten metal into the recesses of their molds, now much larger than any used before, the bronze workers avoided the intricate decorative work, particularly in ornamental drapery, that characterized archaic sculpture. And since marble work now imitated bronze, the general movement toward broad simplicity that is called 'the Severe Style' entered Greek sculpture. Experimentation with more complex and technically more demanding forms of hair style and drapery soon followed. But a stylistic current had been set in motion which we can appreciate in the nude Zeus of Artemision (illustrated on p. 82) and the draped Delphi Charioteer (illustrated on p. 83). It is interesting to observe how the old decorative forms, such as we find on the Siphnian Treasury Frieze at Delphi from about 525 (illustrated on pp. 78 and 107), persist in painting (which we know through the medium of vase-painting), and are only gradually replaced by the simpler 'severe' and the classical style.

[4] And also by R.R. HOLLOWAY, 'Poseidonia-Paestum: relazioni tra monetazione d'argento e monetazione di bronzo', *La Monetazione di Bronzo di Poseidonia-Paestum*, Atti del Terzo Convegno del Centro Internazionale di Studi Numismatici, 1971, p. 139.

[5] R. R. HOLLOWAY, *A View of Greek Art*, Providence, 1973.

At the same time, the Greek artist was bringing to fruition his ambition to create a visually convincing imitation of the human body. It is this fundamental aim expressed in the work of generations of Greek artists that culminated in the classical art of Phidias and his followers at Athens and in the contemporary school of Argos led by Polykleitos. It also provoked the complaints of Plato, whose remarks in the Tenth Book of the *Republic* show how deep-seated was the attachment to an archaic art which made symbols that did not disguise themselves in the appearance of the transient moment. The new classical figure, of which the coin of Croton illustrated on p. 84 provides a good example, overcame the tendency toward static immobility that affected even such powerful designs as the archaic Poseidon at Poseidonia. But what was gained from an easy posture and the suggestion of the figure turning, even if slightly, through space, was a loss for the symbolic force of the coin type. And it is for this reason that designs like that of the Poseidonia Poseidon continued throughout the history of their coinages, modified only in their anatomical details.

The classical figure type, supported by structural drapery or relying on the undraped nude, tended toward a state of hesitation which easily became a state of placidity. The solution of the fifth-century artist to overcome this incipient weakness was to utilize drapery for animation. The decorative effect of archaic drapery was in a sense reborn, and the result was the florid style typified by the figures of the Nike temple parapet in Athens (illustrated on p. 81). Coin images, more than those of sculpture or surviving vase painting, show that the florid style of drapery was matched by florid treatment of the hair which began, however, during the early classical period, only to be amplified by developments in drapery some thirty years later.

The creation of the classical figure was accompanied by an accomplishment, no less significant, but largely unrecorded in the remains of ancient art. This development was the representation of convincing visual space around the human figure. One may examine the sculptural scenes known from classical temples (the Parthenon in particular) without discovering a trace of this achievement. It is reflected in a crabbed way in the reliefs of a provincial heroon in the semi-Greek region of Lycia in Asia Minor (Gjölbaschi-Trysa). But even at the beginning of the classical period the expansion of spatial sense and spatial representation comes before us in the central scene of the Tomb of the Diver at Poseidonia, the only painting, save fragments, to have been preserved from a Greek city of the fifth century B.C. (illustrated on p. 85). Otherwise, we must rely on literary descriptions of lost ancient paintings, and their reflection in vase-painting. Verbal description, however, is especially weak in conveying any spatial sense, and vase-painting is a medium peculiarly ill adapted, because of its curving surface and tonal limitations, to the reproduction of spatial compositions. However, painting and representational pictorial space are a constant influence in South Italian coinage. The seated Heracles of Croton, the

Pan of Pandosia, the river god Acheloos and the Apollo of Metapontum, and the dolphin-riders and horsemen of Tarentum exist in a surrounding space, explicitly detailed, or implied with a minimum of detail.

The influence of such pictorial elements is not restricted to the coinages of South Italy. The Syracusan and Catanian masters of the late fifth century, and especially Euainetos, created images of the chariot race course for coins with a spatial sense that surpasses the South Italian achievements (we must recall, however, that the Sicilian coins were normally tetradrachms, more than twice the size of the normal South Italian major denomination). In Crete there are the remarkable issues with Europa and Zeus as a bull struck at Gortyn. But the introduction of spatial effects surrounding the types of South Italy is such a constantly recurring aspect of these coinages that special circumstances seem to be at work. And these circumstances must derive from the artistic milieu of Magna Graecia.

The art of Magna Graecia is most imperfectly known, especially in the classical age of the fifth and fourth centuries B.C. The materials employed for sculpture are in part to blame. There is no native marble, although importation was less of an expense and problem than has often been asserted. Ships coming west from Greece for South Italian cereal crops could have been ballasted with marble shipments, and sculptors did turn to other materials, limestone and bronze. But the South Italian limestones can be destroyed by weathering, while bronze falls prey to the melting pot. Fate has also been unkind to the recovery of South Italian sculpture. For example, marble figures from the famed temple of Hera Lacinia at Croton were excavated under private initiative in the nineteenth century and then lost. But what remains is impressive, from the fifth century the marble head of Apollo from the Temple of Crimisa (between Sybaris and Croton), the seated goddess from Tarentum now in Berlin (illustrated on pp. 86-87) and the striding bronze Poseidon from Ugentum discovered in 1963. However, enumeration of these masterpieces suggests a problem in measuring the importance of Italic Greek art, for neither the Poseidon or the Tarentum goddess is at all typical of the dominant regional style based on a tradition of terracotta and limestone sculpture[6]. Moreover, no South Italian sculptor achieved international prominence except Pythagoras of Rhegium, who seems to have immigrated there from Samos, the island off the coast of Asia Minor, while major monuments, such as the Tarentine dedications at Delphi and Olympia, were entrusted to artists of the homeland (in these cases Onatas of Aigina and Ageladas of Argos). A similar picture of regional taste modified by the influence of foreign artists will meet us in the coinage of the area.

[6] R. R. HOLLOWAY, *Influences and Styles in the Late Archaic and Early Classical Greek Sculpture of Sicily and Magna Graecia*, Publications de l'Institut supérieur d'archéologie et d'histoire de l'art de l'Université catholique de Louvain, 1975.

In the fourth century, only one city has significant sculptural material: Tarentum, where there are numerous relief fragments from late fourth century tombs, and some sculpture in the round. The minor arts of the area, terracotta figurines and small bronzes, are probably better known than large scale sculpture. Bernard Ashmole has used these to discuss the style of coins, and his observations will be examined in respect to individual coins.

In one field, however, the artists of Magna Graecia were preeminent in the late fifth and fourth century. This field is painting, and the leading South Italian master was Zeuxis. Although Heraclea, the city of his birth, might possibly be the city of that name on the Black Sea, it is generally agreed that he was a South Italian since he was said to have studied with the Sicilian Damophilos and since one of his most famous paintings was the Helen at Croton.

The few passing remarks remaining in ancient literature about his style suggest that Zeuxis made great advances in endowing his figures with illusionistic verisimilitude. So much appears from the otherwise ridiculous anecdotes of the painted grapes which deceived the birds and more serious but briefer mentions of Zeuxis' attention to the effects of linear perspective and perspective effects of light and shade. At the same time the artist was engaged in developing spatial effects. So much is clear from the lengthy description that Lucian wrote of his painting 'The Centaur Family' (*Zeuxis*, 3). In addition to the treatment of the bodies (which Lucian found provocative in the case of the combination of mare and human beauty in the female centaur) the interest of the painting arose from the interaction of the male centaur, half hidden behind a hillock, and his mate and children reclining on the grass below to whom he is showing off a lion cub. The description 'Figures Relaxing in a Landscape' could be applied to a large number of representations that have come down to us from fourth-century Italy (for example the Tarentine amphora, illustrated on p. 88). For the most part, the landscape elements have to be restored by the mind to vase-painting scenes, but one precious source preserves an idea, without the coloristic effects, of this kind of painting. The piece in question is the bronze Ficoroni cista from Palestrina south-east of Rome (illustrated on p. 89). The scene of the cista is the pause in the voyage of the Argonauts and their meeting with king Amykos of Thrace, who has lost his boxing bout with Polydeuces and is bound to a tree awaiting his death. The figures at ease in their landscape setting recall the description of Zeuxis' painting of the centaurs.

One further general topic must detain us before examining individual coins. This is the question of the historical significance of coin types. Traditionally, numismatic scholarship has sought connection between type, especially at the moment of a type change, and the history of the issuing city. Recently, however, the Belgian scholar Léon Lacroix has vigorously challenged this assumption, emphasizing the mythological subject matter of the types and their appropriateness to the mythological traditions of the individual cities[7]. As an example of the difference in interpretation one may take the fourth century 'supplication' gold of Tarentum (illustrated on p. 89), which has the reverse type of an infant raising his hand in gesture to a seated Poseidon. This type has traditionally been associated with the appeal of Tarentum to Sparta for assistance in the Lucanian wars of the mid-fourth century, and specifically with the appeal which led to the expedition of Archidamas in the 340's. The presence of Poseidon representing Sparta is explained by Evans as an allusion to the Poseidon of Taenaron in Laconia whose cult was also maintained in Tarentum[8]. Lacroix wishes to interpret the type on a purely mythological level, the supplication of the infant Taras to his father Poseidon leading to the establishment of the colony. However, the case of Anaxilas' mule coinage issued after his Olympic victory shows that contemporary reference was made by coin types, and since in ancient Greece mythology was so often the language of history, the presence of different levels of meaning in the coin type is altogether logical.

The coins of Magna Graecia of the classical age are, therefore, singularly important in the history of art. Representing a rich segment of the Greek world which has left us so little major art, they have close connections to the utterly perished painting of Zeuxis and Greek painting's achievements in the portrayal of visual space[9]. In their types, moreover, there is tension between the traditions of archaic art and the energy of the classical style. And even through the oblique language of mythology, they may be interpreted as historical voices from a region of Greece where history is so often silent.

[7] L. LACROIX, *Monnaies et colonisation dans l'Occident grec*, Académie royale de Belgique, Classe des lettres, etc. Mémoires ser. 2, vol. 58, fasc. 2, 1965.

[8] A. EVANS, 'The "Horsemen" of Tarentum', p. 67.

[9] Now discussed by V. J. BRUNO, *Form and Color in Greek Painting*, New York, 1977.

The guilloche border of the obverse of the first of our Tarentine coins (illustrated on p. 90) shows its close relationship to the preceding incuse issues of Tarentum. The dolphin rider appeared in earlier series, but with him here is a new type, the seated figure with distaff and kantharos.

This coin raises several problems in the reading and interpretation of Greek coin types. The dynamic simplicity of the Greek coin type is typical of the clarity of meaning that the image was so obviously meant to embody. This clarity of meaning, however, was one that could be lost within generations and give rise to the learned antiquarianism to which modern interpretations, often far more clever than sensible, are a direct heir. So, in this case, the youth on the dolphin may represent either of two personages. The first is the local and mythological figure Taras, derived from the name of the river near the city. The second is Phalanthos, the leader of the Spartan colony in the eighth century B.C. Aristotle, writing on the constitutional history of the Tarentines in the fourth century B.C. (fr. 590 Rose) calls the dolphin rider Taras. Aristotle was probably not familiar with coins like the one before us here but had handled the later Tarentine issues where the dolphin rider is joined with a horseman as the obverse type. Aristotle may have done no more than read the legend of these later issues, which accompanies the dolphin rider, and assumed that the dolphin rider was Taras himself. One cannot say what he would have made of a coin such as these early issues in which the legend accompanies both the elderly seated hero and the youthful dolphin rider. At the sanctuary of Apollo at Delphi, however, there was a sculptural group, contemporary with our coin, a victory monument made for the Tarentines by the great sculptor Onatas of Aegina. It consisted of statues of foot soldiers and horsemen, and Opis the king of the Iapygians (who had come to the aid of Tarentum's troublesome neighbors the Peucetians). King Opis was shown slain in the fight and standing over him the Tarentine heroes Taras and Phalanthos. Together with them, clearly to identify one of the two, was a dolphin and Pausanias, the antiquarian guidebook writer of the second century A.D. to whom we are indebted for our knowledge of the monument, states that the dolphin belongs to Phalanthos, (*Description of Greece*, 10.13.10), one of those lucky survivors of shipwreck who have been kept afloat by helpful dolphins. We might recall that Phalanthos was the leader of a band of settlers belonging to a single generation, which was born and grew up during the prolonged absence of the Spartan army. The suspicion thus drawn on their parentage led to their relegation to an inferior social position and eventual emigration. It is therefore logical to see Phalanthos as the youthful dolphin rider[1]. The gesture of the rider conforms to the

---

[1] For a summary of views on this problem see A. Stazio, 'Aspetti e momenti della monetazione Tarantina', *Taranto nella Civiltà della Magna Grecia*, Atti del decimo convegno di studi sulla Magna Grecia, Taranto, 1970, pp. 148-181.

specific Greek iconography of prayer or expression of gratitude, shown by extending both arms with the palm away from the body[2].

The seated hero must be Taras, an ancient spirit of the Tarentine territory Hellenized in mythological accounts as the son of a Cretan father and native mother. He is represented in the pose adopted by gods as well as heroes, among coins notably by the Zeus of Aitna (illustrated on p. 91) shown on the unique tetradrachm in Brussels belonging to the inauguration of this new city (Catane renamed) by Hieron of Syracuse in the 470's[3]. The hero holds a kantharos. This wine cup is the particular mark of Dionysos but is appropriate to any divine or semi-divine figure to show his right to a libation of wine. The distaff of coiled wool held in the other hand has occasioned some discussion. What is a hero doing with a woman's distaff as if to display some strange hermaphroditic character? The distaff, however, is very possibly a reference to the textile industry of Tarentum based on extraction of dye from shellfish caught in Tarentum's harbor. The seated figure of Taras might be thought to be based on a cult statue, such as the superb marble figure of a goddess which was brought to Berlin from Tarentum early in this century (illustrated on pp. 86-87). But, like the Aitnean god whose thin vine staff and feathery thunderbolt are thoroughly unsculptural, it is more likely to be based on a monumental painting.

The dolphin rider, however, may have been inspired by a statue. We know that such an image stood in the agora of Tarentum, although the date of the statue is unknown and the late antique commentator on the *Georgics* of Virgil to whom we owe this information (Probus on *Georgics* 2.197) has transferred the story of the shipwreck and consequently the identity of the dolphin rider to the hero Taras.

The coin, therefore, is a drama between the images of the two faces. Phalanthos, the Spartan colonist, approaches the ancient hero Taras seeking his protection in establishing the Greek colony on Italian soil. The actual settlement was hardly carried out in a pacific manner, the Greeks storming the native settlement at Tarentum, when, after setbacks and disappointments, the prediction of the Delphic oracle was fulfilled by Phalanthos' wife sobbing in despair at the apparent failure of the mission. Since her name, Aithra, signified the open sky, and the oracle had spoken of rain from a cloudless heaven foretelling success, the Greeks took courage and stormed the town. But in later times the indigenous hero

---

[2] «Entweder werden beide Arme mit nach aussen weisender innerer Handfläche zum Himmel emporgehoben oder die eine, meistens die rechte Hand wird flach vor die Brust gelegt oder mit Innenfläche nach aussen weisende erhoben, jedoch sind die Gestalten stets stehend wiedergegeben», G. NEUMANN, *Gesten und Gebärden in der Griechischen Kunst*, Berlin, 1965, p. 78. The palms are not turned supine as in the incorrectly restored 'Praying Boy' in Berlin.

[3] A second tetradrachm of Aitna with a different obverse type (Athene driving a quadriga and crowned by Victory) has been published by C. BOEHRINGER, 'Hieron's Aitna und das Hieroneion', *Jahrbuch für Numismatik und Geldgeschichte*, vol. 18, 1968, pp. 67-98.

and the Greek colonist were reconciled so that one could appear as an adventurous youth appealing to a dignified elder.

This kind of dramatic representation involving separated figures is typical of Greek art in the early fifth century B.C. Plentiful examples exist in Athenian painted pottery, for example, the vase, nearly contemporary with our coins, made by the anonymous artist now called the Berlin Painter and now in the collection of the Antikenmuseum, Basel (illustrated on pp. 92-93). Here Athene, on one side, pours a libation, intended for Heracles, who holds out his cup on the other face of the vase.

The contrast between youth and age seen in this coin is also typical of the time, and was used with great effect, for example, in the sculptures of the most important Greek temple of this period, the Temple of Zeus in the Sanctuary at Olympia (dedicated in 458 B.C.) where one finds the contrast between the youthful and aged heroes of the east pediment (Pelops and Oinomaos) and other instances of the same comparison of age in the pediments and metope cycle (Labors of Heracles).

The double relief issues of Tarentum, which begin with this coin, thus mark a conceptual advance over the incuse issues, which initially showed one divinity, or the second stage of the coinage, which had the dolphin rider Phalanthos joined by a chariot wheel or a hippocamp as reverse type. Variations of the relation between obverse and reverse multiply as time goes on. In a later stage of the series under discussion both heroes are seated and Phalanthos assumes much of his predecessor's character. He is seated, and holds a staff and distaff.

The hero on the dolphin of our second Tarentine coin (illustrated on p. 95) is joined by a forceful youthful male head. The heads of three dies of this series have necklaces, and this had led Cahn to interpret the entire group as female[4]. The aspect of the image before us here is clearly male, however, and necklaces are not unknown for men, the early *kouroi* statues of the beginning of the sixth century among them. Consequently, I prefer to identify the whole group as male.

Bernard Ashmole has commented on this head from an artistic point of view and finds its closest associations with Tarentine terracottas and with works of art from the Greek Peloponnesos, notably the small bronze head in Boston, from Sparta (illustrated on p. 95)[5]. This latter comparison would give support for artistic ties between Tarentum and her mother city. However, it is difficult to be satisfied with a comparison like this which relies more on the common photographic plane of the image than any real similarities between the pieces. On the basis of hair style the Spartan head belongs

---

[4] CAHN, 'Early Tarentine Chronology'.

[5] B. ASHMOLE, 'Late Archaic and Early Classical Greek Sculpture in Sicily and South Italy', *Proceedings of the British Academy*, vol. 20, 1934, pp. 91-122.

to the end of the sixth century, but its eyes still retain the wide expression of works made fifty years before. The prominent eye of the coin image has a contemporary graphic source, reflected in vase painting. This type of head is also present in *kouroi* of the period 480-460, among which the Ephebe of Agrigentum and the so-called Kritias boy of the Athenian Acropolis are most easily comparable because of the common hair style. But the close ties of the coin image remain with graphic art.

Who is represented in the coin head? Perhaps youthful Phalanthos, the dolphin rider of the reverses. This is conjecture, but attention is drawn to the head by the round frame in which it is sent. At this date it is unlikely that we have to do with a shield image, which became an honorific art form especially for portraits in Hellenistic and Roman times. But a dedicatory round image made for suspension, such as the splendid marble piece with a female head from Melos (illustrated on p. 94), is possibly the inspiration of the border used here.

The artistic richness of the Tarentine coinage during the two and one-half centuries of its span from the mid-fifth century to the time of Hannibal's invasion of Italy drew the attention of Sir Arthur Evans in a monograph ('The Horsemen of Tarentum') which also established the chronological sequence of groups followed today. Immediately after the series of reverse heads within a circle there follows a head within an olive wreath (illustrated on p. 96). This image deserves more than passing attention because it is typical of stylistic tendencies in South Italy of the mid-fifth century, notable at Velia, Terina and especially at Cumae in Campania. The head has a dry angularity emphasized by its abrupt nose line which is more easily appreciated because of the contrast with the flexible line of the olive wreath. In many ways it seems to be a predecessor of Roman denarii of the second and first century B.C. and may, in this way, reflect a slight Italic element in the taste of Magna Graecia. In coin art, however, this current was to be submerged by Sicilian, especially Syracusan (or as others would prefer, direct Athenian) influence at the end of the fifth century.

The following illustration (p. 96), representing Evans' Period I, displays the dolphin rider in a spatial setting of plume-like waves. This type is important testimony to the influence of the awakening of interest in visual space after the middle of the fifth century. On the reverse, a horseman, apparently carrying a lance at rest, introduces the type that was to remain the constant companion of the dolphin rider throughout the long history of the Tarentine mint. The next coin (illustrated on p. 97) brings us to the end of the fifth century. The vaulting rider appears to come from an equestrian display, while the dolphin-riding hero is also armed, in a pose possibly borrowed from representations of the Nereids, mounted on hippocamps, bearing his arms to Achilles. The next coin (illustrated on p. 97) introduces what Evans saw as an artistic climax in the Tarentine coinage. The twisting figure of the dolphin rider ushers in this period of artistic maturity, which Evans also connected to the work of a school of die engravers identified by abbreviated signatures on the coins. One of these, on the next piece illustrated here (p. 98), was ΚΑΛ. A colleague's initial appears on the obverse, Φ. The problem of these signatures will be discussed more fully at the end of this account. The nude figure seen in the act of bridling a horse is representative of the most brilliant figure style of the fourth century B.C. known in sculptural monuments such as the 'Stele from the Ilissos' in Athens (illustrated on p. 99) and typical of the work of Praxiteles. Tarentine coins with an eagle in the field belong to a short period, which Evans connected with the expedition of Alexander the Molossian (uncle of Alexander the Great) to aid the South Italian Greeks in the late 330's (illustrated on p. 100)[6]. The beautifully proportioned armed horseman adopts a pose of combat. Finally, from the early third century we illustrate a coin which makes explicit the aspirations of this long series (p. 101). Victory leads the warrior horseman, while the acrobatic or agonistic function of the horseman in earlier issues is transferred to the dolphin rider who vaults nimbly across the waves.

To these years belong the most majestic examples of Tarentine gold coinage. We have already had occasion to comment on the historical context of the 'Supplication Gold' issued at the time of Tarentine appeals for military aid from Greece, which is reflected particularly in the scene of Poseidon and the infant Taras on the reverse of the coin (illustrated on p. 89). The obverse of a second gold stater, which bears the name of Alexander the Molossian but which was minted at Tarentum, has a noble head of Zeus (illustrated on p. 102). The origin of this conception of the father of gods and men lies in the gold and ivory cult statue made by Phidias for the temple of Olympia in Elis in the 420's B.C., over a generation after the building of the temple itself. Bronze coins of Elis issued under the Roman Empire give a vague idea of the head of Zeus, and the fortunate discovery at Cyrene and at Civita Castellana in Italy of possible sculptural reproductions of the work assists still further in recapturing the impression of Phidias' last masterpiece (illustration on p. 103)[7]. In the Tarentine Zeus one sees the fourth century's elaboration of the Phidian prototype.

---

[6] See recently on Tarentine gold G. K. JENKINS, 'Note sur quelques monnaies d'or de Tarente', *Bulletin du Cercle d'Études Numismatiques*, vol. 11, no. 1, 1974, pp. 2-7.

[7] Skepticism regarding this equation is expressed by P. MINGAZZINI, 'Lo Zeus di Dresda, lo Zeus di Cirene, lo Zeus di Falerii, e lo Zeus di Fidia', *Annuario della Scuola Archeologica di Atene*, vol. 47-48, 1969-70, pp. 71-84.

RHEGIUM

The first Rhegian coin to be discussed here (illustrated on p. 104 above) was struck during the same decade that saw the erection of the Parthenon. The series to which it belongs, however, was introduced in 461, and the seated figure of the reverse maintains the angularity of human figures of what is called 'the Severe Style'. But the Rhegians were not to allow their coinage to fall behind the advances in representation for long, and immediately after the group to which this coin belongs there begins the work of the engraver called by Herzfelder 'The Master of the Classical Iokastos' who brought the figure abreast of Phidian innovations (p. 104 below).

His coin reflects the style of the Parthenon and can be compared with the seated divinities of the Parthenon Ionic frieze (illustrated on p. 105). The same feeling of a relaxed seated posture is there (although it in no way weakens the powerfulness of the body) and the drapery, largely tight and linear in earlier issues, is developed with less taut overfolds through the use of balancing triangles. The figure has become youthful (a warning to anyone who would overemphasize age as a factor in identifying Greek mythological figures). And of note for the history of graphic art, the stool is now rendered in foreshortening so that the far legs are represented. The coin type, however, is the same, and to interpret it one must return to the moment of its introduction.

The types were introduced in 461 B.C. when the sons of the tyrant Anaxilas were driven from the city and a new government established. These were years of general change when the dynasties that had dominated Sicily for almost a half century, the family of Hieron and Gelon at Syracuse and that of Theron of Acragas, also were driven from power. At Syracuse, these events have left no trace in the coinage series unless one follows Kraay's theory of a date about 460 for the splendid ten-drachm piece usually connected with a literary tradition concerning a coin of such value, known as the Damareteion after Gelon's wife Damarete and struck soon after 480[1]. At Catane, a city which recaptured its ancient identity (Hieron had changed its name to Aitna) and at Naxos the liberation of the 460's resulted in the inauguration of distinguished coin series. At Naxos the head of Dionysos is the obverse type and a satyr seated on the ground with a wine cup to his lips provides the reverse. Both this piece and the tetradrachm of the Aitna series in Brussels with a bald satyr's head for the obverse type and a seated Zeus on the reverse (illustrated on p. 91) seem to be the work of a single outstanding artist called the 'Aitna Master'[2].

[1] C. M. KRAAY, *Greek Coins and History*, London, 1969. The suggestions of S. MAZZARINO ('Documentazione Numismatica e Storia Syrakousana del V secolo a.C.' in *Athemon, Scritti di Archeologia e di Antichità in onore di Carlo Anti*, Florence, 1955, pp. 41 ff.) were cogently answered by G. K. JENKINS, *The Coinage of Gela*, Antike Münzen und Geschnittene Steine II, Berlin, 1970, p. 67.

[2] Discussed by R. R. HOLLOWAY, 'Damarete's Lion', *American Numismatic Society, Museum Notes*, vol. 11, 1964, pp. 1-11.

The effect of political events on the Rhegium coinage was different still. The obverse type looks back to the earliest double relief types of Rhegium (illustrated on p. 106). The city's incuse series (man-headed bull) must have been a brief experiment because it is represented by a single unique specimen and Rhegium's relations, numismatic as well as political, were as much influenced by Sicily, just across the Straits of Messina, as by South Italy. It has been customary to regard the Rhegium lion's head as a development of the coin type of Samos, which displayed the head of a lion's pelt, laid flat with the cheeks spread apart. The Samian type was used in the west in the years after 494 when a band of Samians, fleeing the disastrous conclusion of the Ionian Revolt against the Persian Empire, captured Messina (illustrated on p. 106). Through his intrigue with the Samians (whom he expelled from Messina early in the 480's) Anaxilas, tyrant of Rhegium, gained control of Messina as well. The earliest double relief coinage of Rhegium, a true lion's head seen from above combined with the reverse type of a calf's head, is repeated at Messina, and both series have therefore been considered to be related to the rule of the Rhegian tyrant (illustrated on p. 108). The two series, however, are not identical in all respects because at some time during the striking of the Rhegian calf's head series the denominations in which the coinage was issued were changed from those of the Euboic-Chalcidian system to those of the Attic-Sicilian system[3]. Consequently, the Rhegium calf's head series appears to have been struck over a longer time than its Messinian counterpart. It would be possible to reconstruct the history of the coinage so that the first lion's head/calf's head types at Rhegium were parallel to the early coinage of Messina (issued while it retained its original name of Zankle with the unusual type of a dolphin swimming within the sickle-shaped harbor of the city). Anaxilas' advent would then be marked by the introduction of the Attic-Sicilian tetradrachm coinage at Rhegium (though maintaining the lion's head/calf's head types) while his Samian henchmen at Messina issued their lion's pelt/prow coins on the same system. The expulsion of the Samians and the unification of rule under Anaxilas would then see the introduction of the lion's head/calf's head coinage to Messina. At a later moment there follow the biga/hare types which commemorated Anaxilas' victory at the Olympic Games (illustrated on p. 110).

This disgression has shown that it is not necessary to derive the Rhegium lion's head from the Samian pelt. And in choosing the type in 461 the Rhegians returned to an emblem already in use before the rise of Anaxilas, thus demonstrating their anti-tyrannical feelings and their return to a traditional government[4].

[3] From a drachm of about 5.70 gr. to a tetradrachm of ca. 17.00 gr. implying a drachm of 4.25 gr., unless the earlier coin be considered a third of the 17.00 gr. coin.

[4] The reconstruction of the Messina and Rhegium coinage outlined above differs somewhat from that proposed in the authoritative article of Sir Stanley Robinson, 'Rhegion, Zankle-Messana and the Samians', *Journal of Hellenic Studies*, vol. 66,

By divorcing the lion's head from the Samian pelt, however, we raise the problem of the invention of this memorable coin type. The profile view is almost inseparable from archaic Greek graphic art. But this lion's head has little of graphic work about it. It is perhaps the most sculptural Greek coin type, not in the sense that it imitates sculpture in graphic form, but that it has a sculpture-like height of relief. This gives the Rhegium type its intense power, but makes its invention all the more difficult to assess.

The most familiar use of the lion's head in Greek art of this period was as the plastic form of the waterspout along the roofs of Greek temples and other public buildings. But the Rhegium lion's head does not seem to have been inspired by any of these (there are especially notable series from Himera, Syracuse, and Acragas in this period, as well as from Caulonia and Metapontum in South Italy), which, moreover, were seen from below. It is likewise unrelated to the feline head of Greek sixth-century coins, especially the heraldic issues generally attributed to Athens. There is something of a plastic self-sufficiency about the type. It may be compared to the lion of Cybele in the north frieze of the Siphnian Treasury at Delphi of about 525 (illustrated on p. 107) but also suggests an embossing such as we find on Greek armor of the priod, and in this case suggests a shield device, for which a lion's head (facing in the poorly preserved shield at Delphi) is a frequent choice. Such a boss may be illustrated from a series of miniature shields, made principally if not exclusively at Tarquinia in Etruria, for tomb gifts (illustrated on p. 109). These are a long remove from the protome of the Rhegium coins, but they suggest the connections it may have with lost South Italian Greek metal work, and especially armor.

The English numismatist, Sir Stanley Robinson, collected instances of the relationship between the lion and the god Apollo (whose image accompanies the lion protome after about 420)[5]. This connection may assist in identifying the personage represented on the reverse of the coin. We may begin by noting that the seated figure is placed within a laurel wreath, itself significant of Apolline associations. Various contradictory identifications have been offered for the figure. Most commonly accepted today is Six's idea that he is Iokastos, the mythical founder of Rhegium[6]. In favor of this identification there is the undoubted similarity of the Rhegium coins to Tarentine pieces with a similar seated figure who is

1946, pp. 13-20. Robinson makes the lion's head/calf type Anaxilas' invention beginning with his assumption of power in 494, at the same time as the Samians began their lion's pelt issues at Messina, though without considering the Rhegium lion head artistically dependent on the Samian pelt. Robinson's arrangement, however, is less satisfactory for explaining why the Rhegians went back to the lion's head type in 461.

[5] Cited in note 3, and H. CAHN, 'Löwen des Apollo' in *Kleine Schriften*, Basel, 1975, pp. 17-32.

[6] 'Rhegium-Iocastos', *NC*, ser. 3, vol. 18, 1898, p. 281-285.

probably the oikist Phalanthos or Taras. However, the identification is still conjectural, and the appearance of a snake on one of the dies of the series (Iokastos died of snakebite) is hardly convincing evidence.

Asclepius, the divine doctor and son of Apollo, has been suggested, and this idea would seem to agree with the iconography of the seated physician found in representations of doctors on red-figured Athenian pottery, in votives made by physicians, and their grave monuments[7]. Nevertheless, the diffusion of the cult of Asclepius beyond Epidaurus is a phenomenon of the later fifth century, and it is unlikely that he would have been sufficiently important to appear as a coin type in 460 at Rhegium. Although other hypotheses have been advanced for which there is neither binding proof nor absolute condemning evidence, it is not inappropriate to consider one further suggestion, which has the advantage of suiting the political situation of the coins[8].

The Rhegian constitution was based on the famous laws of Charondas of Catane, a figure lost to us in the mists of the early history of the colonies but one whose legal code was adopted by a number of cities besides his own. The dignified and bearded figure of the Rhegian coins was introduced just at a time when the tyrants had been ejected from the city. In such circumstances it was always customary to claim the restoration of an ancestral constitution, and the lion type of the obverse shows that the coinage was looking back to the issues initiated before Anaxilas. Reference to Apollo, the arbitrator of colonization through the oracle at Delphi, is made by the lion's head and by the laurel wreath of the reverse. And within the laurel wreath, what could the seated figure represent more appropriately than the human arbitrator of conduct of the city, Charondas himself?

The connections with Apollo implicit in the earlier coins of Rhegium were made clear in the new series beginning about 420 which has the head of a youthful divinity wearing a laurel crown who can be no other than Apollo (illustrated on p. 111). In his monograph on the coins of Rhegium, Herzfelder has rightly called attention to the personality of the artists involved in creating the new series. Interestingly enough, the series does not begin with the most distinguished dies. Rather, in the work in the first part of the series (signed by the engraver Kratesippos) the Apollo heads have a slight disproportion between the features and their placement in the head which marks them as derived from some foreign prototype. This aspect of the coinage changes with the beginning of dies by a man identified by Herzfelder as 'the Master of the Rhegium Apollo'. Although Herzfelder does not consider

[7] Collected recently by E. BERGER, *Das Basler Arztrelief*, Mainz, 1970.
[8] Zeus (Eckhel), the leader of a Rhegian boys' choir drowned in a shipwreck (Carello), Demos 'the people', (Raoul-Rochette) and Aristaios, son of Apollo (Head), references in Herzfelder, p. 19.

the piece illustrated here (p. 111) part of his work, it is closely allied and one might even view it as a mature phase of the master's style.

The identification of such key dies and key sets of dies in the history of a coin type has become an important aspect of numismatic research. Through it the artistic articulation and the artistic history of the coinage take their place beside the historical significance of the types and the economic aspects of the issues. Engravers such as the Damareteion Master and the Aitna Master in Sicily, or the creator of the Hera head series for Croton, stand apart as significant innovators. But without the study of their talented imitators, to whom fell the task of maintaining the level of Greek coinages, there can be no appreciation of a series as a whole.

So in this case Kratesippos borrowed the florid type of the youthful Apollo, possibly from the coins of Catane of the 420's (and in particular from the series executed by the master called by Rizzo 'the Leaf Master', illustrated on p. 111)[9]. There may be a common prototype for both, because the Apollo of the first issues of the Chalcidian League in northern Greece issued at the league's capital at Olynthos in the 420's is also comparable. These coins, and not least among them the Rhegium pieces, are of the greatest importance in recording the luxuriant hair which gives such fascination to those images by its contrast to the classical immobility of the face itself. It is the hair that creates the animation of the expression, just as in marble sculpture and in vasepainting, the light, wind-blown and complexly rendered drapery lends vitality to figures in the art of the last two decades of the fifth century. We have lost the bronze statues that might have revealed similar dramatic hair, but a mold for the making of terracotta antefixes found at Buccino near Salerno in 1969 reproduces the luxuriant hair of coin images in a contemporary plastic version (illustrated on p. 113)[10]. The culmination of this movement in Greek art (which elsewhere I have termed 'post-Phidian expressionism')[11] is the facing head of Apollo by Herakleides done for a Catane tetradrachm (illustrated on p. 112) in the same years that the Rhegium Apollo type begins.

Rhegium was sacked by Dionysius I of Syracuse in 386 B.C. and this calamity apparently put an end to the Apollo head coinage in silver save for a brief revival shown by our sixth coin (illustrated on p. 115). The Apollo head of this piece is more easily reconciled with other arts, and it is an

[9] G. E. RIZZO, *Monete Greche della Sicilia antiqua*, Rome, 1946.

[10] One may note the magnificent bearded bronze head from a shipwreck discovered near Reggio Calabria also in 1969 illustrated by G. FOTI, *Il Museo nazionale di Reggio Calabria*, Cava dei Tirreni, 1972, pl. 56 and in *Economia e Società nella Magna Grecia*, Atti del dodicesimo Convegno di Studi sulla Magna Grecia, Taranto, 1972, pl. 31-32.

[11] In *A View of Greek Art*, Providence, 1973.

abbreviation of the kind of Apollo pictured before his temple on a Tarentine red-figured vase fragment (illustrated on p. 114). Just as the florid hairstyle of the late fifth-century Apollo replaced the 'Severe', early classical and Phidian types, so this Apollo has now harmonized his features in a vision of the god that became widespread in Greek coinage and endured throughout the succeeding centuries of antiquity.

POSEIDONIA

The obverse type of the major silver coinage of Poseidonia repeats the standing figure of Poseidon of the incuse issues of the sixth century (illustrated on p. 76). As at Rhegium, the god's nature is expressed by a theriomorphic symbol on the reverse: the mighty bull who shakes the ground like the tremor of the earthquake god himself. The energy of both images is potential. But the imminence of the thrust from Poseidon's trident and the danger of the bull's charge are clearly suggested by the later of the two coins illustrated here (p. 116), on which Poseidon's forward thrust can be measured against the incense burner added in the field of the type while the bull's two forelegs are brought together and his head lowered as if he is meditating a savage charge.

The presence of the complicated incense burner, which is found in well-dated representations of a limited period of time in Attic pottery, on the coin of Dossennos (magistrate or die cutter, in either case not of Greek extraction) has permitted Mme. Zancani to establish its date in the mid or later fourth century[1]. The other piece illustrated here belongs to a time when the original Achaean script of Poseidonia (M for s and $\mathcal{f}$ for i) had not yet been replaced by the Ionic script which became common at the end of the fifth century. A date earlier, in the first half of the fifth century (earlier than Kraay suggests)[2] is possible for this coin.

This Poseidon type begins in the very years that the same figure of a god brandishing his weapon becomes common in the Greek world, especially for Zeus, shown in this pose both on the coins of the Olympian sanctuary and in votive statuettes. Two original bronze statues of the early and mid-fifth century repeat the same type. They are the Zeus or Poseidon from a ship wreck off Cape Artemision in Greece, now one of the major treasures of the National Museum in Athens (illustrated on p. 82), and the recently discovered Poseidon from Ugentum not far from Taranto. It is impossible to say whether this long series of coins reproduces a statue at Poseidonia, adapting its archaic character little by little to later taste. The modification of the type, however, has much to tell us about Greek taste and the Greek concept of tradition in art. The fact is that the type is modernized only up to 'the Severe Style' of the second quarter of the fifth century. It is for this reason that the Artemision Zeus is such a convincing parallel for the anatomy of the Dossennos coin, minted over a century later, while the somewhat heavier proportions of the earlier coin are comparable to versions of the type known from bronze votive statuettes. The folds of the god's mantle or chlamys, at first glance typical of the so-called 'swallow tail' drapery of archaic times, are fully at home in the early classical age, not in the 'Severe

[1] P. ZANCANI-MONTUORO, 'Dossenno a Poseidonia', *Atti e Memorie della Società Magna Grecia*, n.s. vol. 2, 1958, pp. 79-94. I would consider Dossennos a magistrate.

[2] C. M. KRAAY, 'Gli stateri a doppio rilievo di Poseidonia', *Atti e Memorie della Società Magna Grecia*, n.s. vol. 8, 1967, pp. 113-135.

Style' typified by the sculptures of the Olympia Temple but in work of other schools, exemplified for instance by the marble goddess from Tarentum in Berlin [3] and they are common in graphic work such as Athenian red-figured vases.

The modernization of the Poseidon image, therefore, halted in the early to mid-fifth century. This point marks the birth of archaism in Greek art, that is, a recognition that there exist older styles of representation distinct from contemporary preferences but valid in themselves and useful for symbolic contrast with the styles of the present. The style of the Poseidon figure acquired a validity apart from the subject only at this moment. And its perpetuation thereafter shows that it became an element in the personality of the god, ancient and remote as well as powerful and eternal. This development is related to the contrast between youth and age which begins at the same time in Greek art as we have considered in discussing the Phalanthos and Taras coins of Tarentum.

[3] Illustrated on pp. 86-87.

CAULONIA

The obverse type of the coinage of Caulonia, a colony of Croton, shows Apollo in the stance used for Poseidon at Poseidonia (illustrated on p. 117). In his right hand, not visible in this specimen, the god holds his symbol, a laurel branch. His stag appears on both obverse and reverse. The obverse depicts a stag on a base, this being one of the rare occasions in which a coin type of the classical period attempts clearly to reproduce an actual sculpture. The relation of the god to this image presents a problem: the extent to which the field of the coin should be considered visual space. Considering the tendencies in this direction in coins of Terina and Metapontum of the fifth century, this is the most reasonable interpretation of the type. Whether the god himself is meant to be a statue, however, is less clear. As we shall see when examining the coins of Metapontum, indicating the presence of a divinity in his sanctuary does not require a consistent iconography and so is not dependent on physically existing images.

The stag, as he appears on the reverse of the coin, is related to a number of outstanding Greek gems, especially those of the eastern Greek area called 'Greco-Persian'[1]. There is no such stringent connection with a prototype, however, as exists for the lion and deer group on the coins of Velia.

[1] J. BOARDMAN, *Greek Gems and Finger Rings*, London, 1970.

The first issue of a double relief coinage at Metapontum is a silver coin with the figure of the river divinity Acheloos (illustrated on p. 118 above). The position of this coin in the Metapontine series is made certain by the fact that its obverse die was held over from the incuse series. The date at which the change occurred has only emerged in the last fifteen years due to detailed numismatic study of overstrikes, that is, coins restruck for new issues by foreign cities. In most cases the under type is obliterated, but occasionally there are sufficient traces of the old type to permit identification of the under type. To this there is added the evidence of hoards, which document coins taken out of circulation together or gradually accumulated down to a certain moment. By these means the English numismatist Colin Kraay has suggested that the Metapontum double relief series began about 450 B.C.[1] Although not all students of Greek coinage would agree with Kraay's interpretation of the evidence, the artistic aspects of the coins seem to support his conclusions.

The Acheloos type is an innovation in more than one way. It carries a very full legend: the name of the city on the obverse and on the reverse both the name of the god and the word *Athlon* or prize. Belonging to a short series of coins in which a variety of types are introduced, it is likely that both the standing Apollo and Heracles figures illustrated here were minted, as Lenormant suggested, to be given as prizes at athletic games for the god. It is logical that the cult of a river divinity would be important at Metapontum, bordered by the Bradanus and Casuentus rivers, which in the flood season pour down with a torrent collected in their lower Apennine catchment. According to some, Acheloos, the river divinity of Albanian Greece remembered for his passion for Heracles' bride Deianeira and his combat with the hero, was also the father of the Sirens, the temptresses of Odysseus' crew, whose home was in the west. Suggestions that the games may have commemorated a successful anti-malarial drainage project at Metapontum, like similar ideas for a youthful god depicted in the act of pouring a libation on the coins of Selinus, are speculation.

The figure of Acheloos on the coins does not follow the tradition whereby the god was shown as a marine monster with human head, or, more commonly in this period, as a man-headed bull. There is a strong tradition of the latter type in the coin art of Magna Graecia and Sicily beginning at Laos in the incuse series, well known from the coins of Gela in Sicily, and destined for its greatest exploitation in the series of Naples and the other Campanian mints which were beginning about this time. But at Metapontum one feels close to conscious artistic choice, which reduces the theriomorphic content of the figure to the horns and ears of the bull. If the archaic age had visualized the spirits of nature as mighty animal antagonists, the Acheloos of Metapontum is the harbinger of an abandonment of such

---

[1] C. M. KRAAY, 'Caulonia and South Italian Problems', *NC*, series 6, vol. 20, 1960, pp. 53-82.

symbolism and the accommodation of these spirits to the company of gods and heroes in human form. The Acheloos of Metapontum is already past the midpoint on the road to the paternal river gods of Hellenistic and Roman art.

The standing Apollo and Heracles who appear in the same sequence of dies as the Acheloos show a uniform concept of male form (illustrated on p. 118 below and p. 120). Together they are an important document of the development of such figures in art, since they belong to the years immediately preceding the diffusion of the canonic Polykleitan standing figure and his Phidian counterparts.

Accustomed to thinking of Greek art in terms of sculpture, it has been natural for numismatists to believe that these types have sculptural prototypes[2]. This is especially so because Herodotus, who took part in the foundation of Thurii in the 440's, and so almost certainly spoke from personal experience, talks of two statues by the altar of Apollo in the marketplace of Metapontum (*Histories* 4.15). One was dedicated as a result of the bizarre affair involving a man who appeared at Metapontum claiming to be a certain Aristeas of Proconnesos, who had disappeared in his homeland on the Black Sea two centuries before. The stranger called on the Metapontines to erect his statue by order of Apollo. He added that he had formerly been a crow, in which form he had received those instructions from Apollo, perhaps mystifying his auditors even more but also appealing to the widespread belief in the transmigration of souls that had been favored by South Italian Pythagoreanism. The mysterious visitor further stated, perhaps as a last appeal, that Apollo had selected only Metapontum as his Italian home. After consulting the Delphic oracle and receiving favorable comment, the Metapontines erected the two statues, one of Aristeas and one of Apollo.

How great a possibility is there that the Apollo type coin reproduces a statue? This question can be answered by considering closely the representation of the figure. The Apollo has a noticeable displacement of the hip toward the left. The resulting curve in the body is motivated by the distribution of weight on the legs. The right leg has become the true weightbearing leg, while the left leg is flexed and relaxed. All the elements of the pose favored by the mid-fifth century Argive sculptor Polykleitos (the so-called Polykleitan chiasmus) are present, save the imbalancing of the shoulders caused if the chiastic distribution of weight is followed through fully. In the classical Polykleitan stance the shoulder above the free leg rises, while the opposite shoulder is depressed. This pose requires a certain rotation of the body which represents the great advance of a Polykleitan figure over those of the previous generation of sculptors. To the eye of this critic, the Acheloos and the Heracles type definitely do not

---

[2] F. LENORMANT, *La Grande Grèce*, ed. 2, vol. 1, Paris, 1881, p. 127 and accepted by P. W. LEHMANN, *Statues on Coins of Southern Italy and Sicily in the Classical Period*, New York, 1946.

display rotation of the body and the Apollo very little if any. If there were a statuary type involved in the background of the coin type, it should resemble male figures of the 'Severe Style' of the second quarter of the fifth century, such as the bronze statue reproduced by a group of Roman copies known together as the Omphalos Apollo type, which has been called the cornerstone of our knowledge of the style of the period (illustrated on p. 121). But where in the statuary of that generation is the sinuous curve of the coin images? The situation is exactly the same if we inspect the small-scale bronze figures from western Greece which are thought to have a distant relationship to larger sculpture and especially to the work of Pythagoras of Rhegium.

Before taking refuge in the myth of a 'free graphic interpretation', it would be better to look to painting. And in painting there are just the prototypes we are seeking for the Metapontine coin images. These are supplied by an interesting source, the Attic red-figure crater in the Louvre (illustrated on p. 119), name-piece of the painter known as the Niobid Painter, who seems to reproduce, especially in this vase, a painting, or elements of a painting, of the school of Polygnotos, the major painter of the second quarter of the fifth century. It is largely the tiered composition of the figures and the indication of landscape that establishes the similarity between the Niobid Painter's vase and the surviving description of Polygnotos' two monumental paintings, 'the Sack of Troy' and 'the Underworld' in the sanctuary at Delphi (Pausanias, 10.25-31). Our interest, however, is in the individual figure types. The Paris crater has them all. The Heracles of the vase is the Apollo of the coin type. The hero to his right on the vase is the Metapontine Acheloos. And the hero with a spear above the handle of the crater gives us the hand-on-the-hip pose of the Heracles of the coins. And just as is suggested by the coin types, the Niobid Painter's bodies, though almost completely frontal, have a sinuous curve through the abdomen, especially on the side of the free leg. The clear efforts of the coin engravers to bring out the muscles of the chest and abdomen repeat the diagram-like precision of the anatomical renderings of the Niobid painter. The graphic type was transferred to relief, on the Parthenon for example (West Frieze, slab V, figure 9). But the closely connected series of Metapontine coins in all probability depends directly on graphic sources, perhaps a Polygnotan-influenced work in South Italy.

The relation of coin types and painting at Metapontum becomes even clearer in the light of the remarkable type, possibly struck at the end of the fifth century, showing Apollo seated with his lyre (illustrated on p. 122). The grace of the musician, which has something in common with the latest seated figures on the coins of Tarentum, takes on an impressive scale, largely due to the massive lyre. His stool is represented with foreshortening. But most remarkable of all is the spatial feeling given to the design by the laurel bush. This must be the laurel grove of Apollo at Metapontum mentioned by Herodotus. But the god within the grove is not a statue. He is a vision, such as he might have appeared in a painting, but hardly to be confused with a statue in the grove. The vision of the inspired singer had been presented elsewhere, in the scene of Orpheus surrounded by enraptured Thracians on a crater in Berlin (illustrated on p. 123). But it is this same visionary quality of Greek coin art that frees it from slavish imitation of prototypes and makes it possible for it to achieve repeated moments of great impact and originality.

The frontal head becomes a three-quarter view in the treatment of Dionysos on another coin (illustrated on p. 124). ΚΑΛ and ΦΙΛΟ also appear here as marks on the Tarentine coinage. Evans interpreted them as artists' signatures. It is uncertain whether the same is true here, and further whether the same individuals can be referred to in both context. This question is discussed again below (p. 68 ff).

The visionary potentialities of Greek art are well illustrated by another Metapontine coin (illustrated on p. 125). The identification of the obverse type is quite uncertain. In Libya we would have Zeus Ammon, the god of the oasis of Siwa, or Hermes Parammon. The ram's head god at Metapontum could be Apollo Carneius, the Peloponnesian divinity whose cult name means ram *(karnos)* and whose worship was practiced in South Italy, as shown by representation of the cult on red-figured vases probably made at Tarentum. Some support for this view is forthcoming from the bronze statuette discovered in 1966 among votives from the Temple of Apollo, portraying a man bearing a ram on his shoulders. But whatever the identification, it is the majestic interplay of the human and the nonhuman, of logical humanity and instinctive strengh, of the known and the unknown that gives this coin its strange fascination.

Together with the power of invention, Greek coin art kept the ability to adapt types invented elsewhere without loss of their integrity or their powers of suggestion as seen in still another coin of Metapontum (illustrated on p. 126 above). This head of Persephone was made famous by the decadrachms of Euainetos made at Syracuse in the last decade of the fifth century and the years following. It was Euainetos who exploited the development of the elaborate style to the fullest in the intricately entwined hair and grain ears, while balancing this against the classical stereotype of the goddess' features. At Metapontum the type was taken up for this issue, but it is the goddess of the plain of the Bradanus, not the Sicilian lady, whose image and personality adorn the coin.

While influence from the brilliant school of Sicilian coin art centered at Syracuse just before 400 is apparent in the Euainetan prototype of the preceding coin, our next piece (illustrated on p. 126 below) shows the independence with which South Italian engravers could treat the classical head type and in so doing keep alive the distinctively regional quality which one sees best in the fifth-century coins of Terina. The goddess is Victory and so identified by the inscription of the obverse. Once again, the occasion for which she was given exceptional honor in the Metapontine series, no doubt a military success, is unknown.

The helmeted head of the general-statesman acquired its classical form in Cresilas' portrait of Pericles done after the Athenian leader's death in 429, of which Roman copies are preserved. On coins the richness of the relief work on the helmet of a head which we may assume to be Leucippus, the founder of Metapontum, reflects the styles in sculptured armor of the day (illustrated on p. 127). A pair of cheekpieces from a general's parade armor from the valley of the Acris behind Heraclea survives in the British Museum. Their fighting Greeks and Amazons give one some feeling of the detail that would have been worked on the founder hero's equipment. A recent discovery has restored to us a fifth-century bronze original of a helmeted bearded hero. It was discovered in the sea near Rhegium and although it may not have come originally from Magna Graecia, it shows us what was in the mind of the creator of the coin image[3].

[3] Illustrated in G. FOTI, *Il Museo Nazionale di Reggio Calabria*, Cava dei Tirreni, 1972, pl. 57 and in *Economia e Società nella Magna Grecia*, Atti del dodicesimo Convegno di Studi sulla Magna Grecia, Taranto, 1972, pl. 32.

THURII

The foundation of Thurii under Athenian auspices at the edge of the plain of Sybaris in 446 revived the memory of the perished Achaian metropolis. Thurii also represents a likely port of entry for Athenian artistic influence to penetrate southern Italy. From this point of view, the foundation of the new city could not have been better timed, since it followed by only two years the inauguration of the great building program at Athens that included the Parthenon and the other architectural monuments of the Periclean era. Through her empire, which made half the Aegean Greek world dependent states from which talented young men could be drawn to Athens and the building program which gave them work, Athens became the artistic, as she was the intellectual, center of Greece. Much of the splendor of western Greek coinage of the later fifth and fourth centuries is a reflection of the advances made in Athens under Pericles and Phidias. But to what extent Athens directly dominated the artistic life of South Italy in the Phidian age is uncertain. While it is clear that the red-figured pottery industry of the region, which began about the time of the founding of Thurii, was established by Athenian-trained potters and painters, there is too little remaining of sculpture to trace any particular influence. Major painting, moreover, had a western tradition of its own which produced the great Zeuxis just at this time. The problem of connections between Athens and South Italian coin art is complicated by the existence of the master engravers of Sicily who had been well established since archaic times and during the second and third quarters of the fifth century created brilliant series at Leontini and Catane before the emergence of the famous group of engravers centered at Syracuse in the last quarter of the century. The influence of the Sicilian coin engravers was naturally paramount in adjacent areas. Some of these artists may have had Athenian training, but this is a conjecture based largely on the preeminence of Phidian Athens as an artistic center, and equal, if not greater weight, should be accorded the strength of the nearby regional centers.

The types of the Thurian coinage unite Athens with the memory of Sybaris (illustrated on p. 128). The Sybarite bull joins the head of Athene[1]. But as we know from the dedication of an Olympic victor discovered in the Sybarite settlement at Francavilla Marittima, Athene was a major Sybarite goddess, too[2]. In the early stater coinage Athene's helmet is unadorned save for an ivy or laurel crown. But with the issue of the double staters, approaching in size the tetradrachms of Greece and Sicily, the helmet

[1] For the Athene head see E. POZZI, «Riflessi della tipologia monetale Ateniese sulle emissioni delle zecche italiote e siceliote», *La Circolazione della Moneta Ateniese in Sicilia e in Magna Grecia*, Atti del Primo Convegno del Centro Internazionale di Studi Numismatici, 1967, pp. 33-110.
[2] M. W. STOOP and G. PUGLIESE CARRATELLI, 'Tabella con iscrizione arcaica', *Atti e Memorie della Società Magna Grecia*, n.s. vol. 6, 1965, pp. 10-17.

appears decorated with a griffin, or more normally with a figure of Scylla, the mariner-devouring monster, part woman, part dog, and part snake. Such an elaborate helmet ornament seems to reflect the influence of the Athene Parthenos of Phidias, made during the 430's for the new Parthenon, and adorned with an elaborate triple-crested helmet bearing griffins. As mythological guardians of treasure, the griffins appropriately protected the gold and ivory cult statue (which represented a considerable portion of the Athenian state's bullion reserve). The Scylla of the Athene at Thurii may probably be a substitute for the fear-inspiring gorgon of the goddess' leather cloak or aegis which could not appear on a coin image showing only the head. Like the gorgon, the Scylla was calculated to strike terror into the hearts of any enemy of the goddess or the city.

The Sybarite bull also develops a more belligerent attitude on the coins of Thurii. He charges, head lowered, toward an invisible antagonist. The bull's posture reflects artistic studies of the mid-fifth century (such as the famous cow of the sculptor Myron) which have also left a record in the small bronze bull from South Italy in Cleveland (illustrated on p. 129) as well as in the fragments of a Roman reproduction of a full-size bull in bronze in the Capitoline Museum in Rome, those of the Eretrian bull at Olympia, and which have a forerunner in the recently restored gold and silver archaic bull at Delphi[3].

---

[3] P. AMANDRY, 'Statue du toreau en argent', *Etudes Delphiques*, Suppl. no. 4, Bull. de Correspondence Hellénique, 1977, pp. 273-293.

HERACLEA

The concept of Athene as a youthful goddess, almost a girlish admirer of Heracles, is exploited on the metopes of the Temple of Zeus at Olympia, especially in the scene of Heracles and Athene standing by the corpse of the Nemean Lion and the hero's return to the goddess with the birds of Lake Stymphalus. The same idea is at work on the earliest of the coins of Heraclea (illustrated on p. 130), in which a female head crowned with an olive wreath is superimposed on a snake-ringed aegis[1]. On the other face of the coin we find an image of Heracles similar to those employed at Croton, and testifying to the importance of the pictorial prototype, possibly by Zeuxis, that was employed for both.

By far the greater part of the coins of Heraclea show Heracles' encounter with the Nemean Lion. The scene in which the two opponents grapple in an upright position had a long history in Greek art, but the fifth century tended to replace the encounter of an armed Heracles with his victim by a scene taken from the wrestling ground, in which Heracles throttles the lion with a headlock. In two issues at Heraclea a frontal Athene (adapted from Eukleides' facing goddess at Syracuse or an intermediate source) accompanies a representation of the struggle in which Heracles swings back from the beast to deliver a blow with his club (illustrated on p. 131). Our third coin has the more common iconography in which Heracles has put his weapons aside to wrestle the beast into submission (illustrated on p. 132). This seems to be the way in which the episode was depicted on a metope of the Treasury of the Athenians at Delphi at the beginning of the fifth century, and on a metope of the Hephaesteon (the 'Theseum') at Athens begun in 448 B.C., and it is known from gem representations as well as vases and coins of Cilicia and Cyprus. In the coin illustated here, Heracles has all the lithe strength of the athletic figures developed during the fourth century, especially by the sculptor Lysippos, while his opponent is worthy of the fierce lions of Velia. The composition adapted itself easily to a curved space, even more so the variation explored in our fourth coin (illustrated on p. 132), in which Heracles keeps his headlock and, kneeling, prepares to dispatch the lion with his club. This is an open version of the scene as represented on Syracusan gold by the engraver Euainetos (illustrated on p. 133). It was adapted to a sculptural version in a large terracotta antefix in Salerno (illustrated on p. 133). We should restrain any temptation to see the great Syracusan master's name in the letters EY below the group on this coin.

The final type of Heraclea is illustrated on our fifth coin (p. 134). In this figure one can appreciate the modification of pose introduced by the Polykleitan male figures of the fifth century that was quickly adopted throughout Greek sculpture. The weightbearing and free legs and the consequent displacement of the upper body are executed as they were incorporated in Greek art of the fourth century. If we

[1] Recently studied by A. Stazio, 'Contributo allo studio della prima fase della monetazione di Heraclea Lucaniae', *Annali dell'Istituto Italiano di Numismatica*, vol. 12-14, 1965-1967, pp. 77ff.

were dealing with a sculptural piece, the extended arm would mark the desire for penetration of space introduced by the sculptor Lysippos. The presence of the altar, however, as well as our experience with coin art, suggests that the concept of the type is once again pictorial.

The Athene heads of the Heraclea series (illustrated on p. 134)[2] move from the Scylla type already encountered at Thurii, through its variation with the guardian griffin derived ultimately from the Athene Parthenos of Phidias, to the Corinthian helmet with griffin, which, combined with the long hair of the goddess, suggests a prototype in the gold coinage of Alexander the Great, no earlier than 336 (illustrated on p. 135).

[2] Left above is obverse of p. 133 above; right above is obverse of p. 133 below.

CROTON

Despite the attempts which have been made to read Pythagorean interpretations into the coin types of the city where Pythagoras established his philosophical sect in southern Italy, the coins of Croton bear types with obvious reference to Apollo, Zeus, Hera, and Heracles. In the Apolline tripod, perpetuated from the incuse series, the Crotonians developed an enduring symbol of the god who from his sanctuary at Delphi was felt to be the direct leader of colonizing (illustrated on p. 136). In the heroic age of Greece as we know it from Homer, the tripod was already a monumental prize, and excavation in the Greek sanctuaries, especially at Olympia, has brought to light bronze tripods dating to the centuries of the beginning of colonization or earlier. In the eighth and ninth centuries when these basins on stands were dedicated, there were no sculptural dedications, and in impressiveness the tripods challenged the modest buildings of the day. The way in which the tripod became especially prominent at Delphi is shown by the Attic red-figured volute crater by the Cleophon Painter of about 440 B.C., found at Spina at the head of the Adriatic, and depicting a procession to the god seated in his temple (illustrated on p. 137). The oval omphalos before the god's throne identifies the location and two large tripods flank the temple.

A variant of the issue illustrated here (p. 136) emphasizes the monumentality of the tripod by using it as the center of the scene of contest between Apollo and his rival for the Delphic sanctuary, the snake Python. Both the monster and Apollo, assuming the stance of Heracles shooting at his three-bodied antagonist Geryon on the sculptured metope from the Temple of Hephaistos at Athens (The 'Theseum') built during the third quarter of the century, are dwarfed by the tripod.

The sculptural character of the Apollo might lead one to adopt the suggestion that this coin illustrates the sculptural group of Apollo and Python by the sculptor Pythagoras of Rhegium. But as Lacroix pointed out, the Pythagorean group is not known to have been made for Croton. It is not known to have contained a tripod, and if it did, it is unlikely that the god would have been made so small in proportion[1].

The incuse reverses of a number of Crotonian issues have an intaglio eagle, and in the double relief series the eagle becomes the companion type of the tripod. The Crotonian eagles are often shown standing over a stag's head. This may be less the prey of the eagle (as it seems to be of the lion at Velia) than a second symbol of Apollo, thus bringing Apollo and Zeus into relation in the same way they figure in the sculptural decoration of the great Temple in the Sanctuary at Olympia. Heracles is also present in the sculptural decoration of the Olympia temple. Zeus dominates the east pediment (super-

[1] L. LACROIX, *Les reproductions de statues sur les monnaies grecques*, Bibliothèque de la Faculté de Philosophie et Lettres de l'Université de Liège, vol. 116, 1949, pp. 249-251.

58

vising the chariot race of Pelops and Oinomaos), Apollo occupies a similarly central and dominating position on the east pediment (in the midst of the brawl between centaurs and Greeks at the wedding of Peirithoos the Thessalian), and the sculpture of the frieze over the two porches of the temple was given over to the labors of Heracles.

Heracles' quest for the cattle of Geryon in Spain provided the background for legends which brought him to almost every city in the west. At Croton he thus appears as a mythical founder of the city. The coin type is one of particular opulence. The seated hero takes his place in a pictorial space, the relation of which to painting is emphasized clearly by the flames shown burning on the altar (illustrated on p. 138). The concept of the hero at rest was not a new one in Greek art. It derives from the apotheosis of Heracles and his triumphal reception among the gods. By the second quarter of the fifth century it had developed into the scenes of Heracles resting after his individual labors on the metopes of the Temple of Zeus at Olympia. The idea of repose as the height of felicity comes forward in the Phidian age, typified by vase-painting scenes of Heracles enjoying the company of the daughters of Atlas in the Garden of the Hesperides. From the later fifth century the figure of a fatigued hero, possibly Odysseus, is preserved on the plaster impression of a buckle (the original of which was very likely silver) from the Athenian Agora (illustrated on p. 138). In southern Italy the idea of divine leisure is captivatingly expressed by the mysterious Dionysos painted by the Carneiades Painter, as he is called, at Tarentum in the late fifth century (illustrated on p. 88).

The facing head of the obverse of another Crotonian piece (illustrated on p. 139) shows the goddess of one of the most famous sanctuaries of Greek Italy, that of Hera at the Lacinian Cape six miles from Croton. As Livy (24.3, 2-7) describes it, 'Six miles from this noble city was the still more noble sanctuary of Hera Lacinia, venerated by all the surrounding peoples. The grove ringed with thick vegetation and tall pines had a pasture in the center where a herd of every kind of beast sacred to the goddess pastured without shepherd. The different species went their own way to the stall at night, never ambushed by wild beast or trapped by man. The return on the flocks was considerable, and from it there was made and dedicated a solid gold column. Thus the sanctuary was famous for its wealth as well as its holiness. And miracles are reported, as generally in such venerable places. It is said that there is an altar in the porch of the temple whose ashes are never disturbed by any wind'.

It was for this temple that the painter Zeuxis of Heraclea did numerous paintings in the late fifth century. Among these was a Helen which achieved great notoriety in classical authors because it was linked with the anecdote that made him combine the best features of the most beautiful women of Croton in the painting. To some such important source we must look for the prototype of the facing divinity that appears at Croton, Poseidonia, Pandosia, Thurii, in Campania, and in varying forms at

Metapontum and overseas in the early fourth-century coinage of Thessaly and in the coins of the Persian satraps of Cappadocia. It was Lenormant's idea that this must be a painting of Zeuxis, and the suggestion has much to recommend it[2].

Zeuxis is the outstanding artist of the Greek west. His appearance in literary references in the company of such figures as Apollodoros, Parrhasios and Apelles shows the importance of his work, possibly representing the second generation of a succession of painters in the west (his teacher in some sources was reported to have been Damophilos of Himera in Sicily). And this eminence in painting explains the influence which this art exercised on coinage from the middle of the fifth century. From this Hera head one can understand the remark of his contemporary Xenophon (*Oecon.* 10, 1) that he was a painter of fair women.

The Heracles of the reverse continues the tradition of the coin discussed above, while giving it a form which more closely follows the Heracles (Theseus or Dionysos) of the Parthenon's east pediment (illustrated on p. 140). This reclining hero had an influence long after his own day. In Italy the most interesting contemporary plastic version is found on a helmet cheekpiece from Praeneste near Rome (illustrated on p. 141). The suggestion has been put forward that these coins were the source of the revival of the figure in the Renaissance leading to the Adam of Michelangelo on the Sistine Chapel ceiling[3].

The infant Heracles strangling the snakes conjured up to destroy him by the wrathful Hera is the subject of a Crotonian reverse (illustrated on p. 141). The type appeared elsewhere in the Greek world. It is used in Thebes, Heracles' home, and was adopted in the 390's by the Ionian cities in revolt against Persia as the common type of an alliance coinage. It also appears at Tarentum for gold and fractional silver. The type is clearly derived from a painting, as shown by the ground indicated under the infant; it may, in fact, be a detail taken from the painting by Zeuxis of the infant Heracles strangling the snakes in the presence of his mother Alcmene and his foster-father Amphitryon. A much-impoverished reproduction of this painting may exist in three wall decorations at Pompeii[4]. The amulets worn by the child probably contained elements of amber, coral and possibly a wolf's tooth, all specially recommended for children's protection from malevolent forces.

[2] F. LENORMANT, *La grande Grèce*, ed. 2, vol. 2, Paris, 1881, p. 222. The influence of graphic art was defended, in the face of Furtwängler's emphasis on relations to Attic sculpture, especially in the work of 'Φ' at Terina, by A. J. EVANS, 'The Artistic Engravers of Terina and the Signature of Euainetos on its Later Didrachm Dies', *NC*, ser. 4, vol. 12, 1912, pp. 20-62.

[3] F. WALTON, 'Adam's Ancestor', *Archaeology*, vol. 13, 1960, pp. 253-258.

[4] A version current in Attic red-figured pottery from the time of the Berlin Painter (Louvre stamnos G 192, B. PHILIP-PAKI, *The Attic Stamnos*, Oxford, 1967, pl. 63) showed the infant battling the snakes on a bed.

The stater of Pandosia of about 400 B.C. is, to quote Head, 'one of the most exquisite productions of any Greek mint' (illustrated on p. 142). The coinage of Pandosia was always closely connected with that of the coastal cities (the early issue has the river god Cratis given the pose of the Acheloos at Metapontum) and this coin is clearly related to the Hera Lacinia and Heracles pieces of Croton. The goddess at Pandosia, however, surpasses the Crotonian figure. There is an energy, richness, and a touch of fascination about this version of the facing goddess, first developed perhaps at Croton and perfected for Pandosia's issue.

The jewelry of the goddess is rich and detailed. Her necklace is composed of acorns evidently made of light gold or silver balls tightly strung so that they refuse to lie flat and stand out from her neck. The earring is a cluster of five globes below a palmette. The crown has two hippocamps, as do more elaborate versions of the type at Croton.

The windblown locks of the Pandosia goddess clearly show that she depends on inspiration from painting, though the immediate inspiration may have been Kimon's Arethusa head on the coins of at Syracuse. And the reverse type again corresponds to the subject of a known painting of Zeuxis (Pliny, *Historia Naturalis*, 35, 62). Pan seated in a landscape, however, was clearly a traditional subject since it appears as the reverse type of a rare issue of Messina in Sicily shortly after the middle of the fifth century. Although the scene corresponds to those of the Crotonian Heracles reverses, the figure of Pan dominates the landscape surrounding him to a lesser degree, while the three planes represented by the dog, the god and the herm give a greater sense of pictorial depth. Pan also looks out in full face from the scene.

The Pan scenes of the fractional silver and bronze issues accompanying the larger didrachm stay closer to the Heracles type of Croton, especially the bronze on which Pan starts his hound in the same pose and with the same outstretched arm of the Crotonian reclining Heracles (illustrated on p. 144).

Other echoes of our seated Pan are to be found in the cheekpiece of a helmet now in the Fogg Museum, Harvard University (illustrated on p. 143) and in a terracotta plaque from Medma in Reggio Calabria (illustrated on p. 144).

TERINA

The coins of Terina are a series of great thematic consistency as well as artistic variation. The obverse dies of the group illustrated here, which except for the first and last were struck during the second half of the fifth century, illustrate the tendencies toward stylistic variation of the normally stereotyped classical head. Whether these movements are conscious attempts at variation or whether they represent an unconscious provincialism is a question debated by all writers on western Greek art. The coinage of Terina is especially valuable in this respect because of the evident technical accomplishment of its die cutters. It may be said, therefore, that their work aimed at imparting personality to the coin type, as is obvious if their work is compared to the Athene heads of Thurii, Velia and Heraclea. The results of these tendencies are deviations from the standard of beauty we have come to expect from Phidian Athens and fifth century Greece.

Some of the heads are thin and angular, some are fleshy and even coarse. Between the two extremes, however, there is a great feeling of personality and charm. In some cases the Terina heads parallel a kind of taste seen in other south Italian art, characterized by the full and fleshy concept of the human features and especially prominent in Tarentine sulpture of this period. Another group of obverse heads has tendencies toward an angularity of execution, equally characteristic, but more natural perhaps to the gem cutter or die engraver than to the sculptor or painter.

On the basis of this complete die study of the Terinian coinage, Regling divided its artistic history into three phases. The first period comprises the early issues such as the first two illustrated here (illustrated on p. 145). There follows, in the last quarter of the fifth century, two periods of activity associated with the signatures Φ and Γ respectively.

Our third and fourth specimens are examples of Φ's work (illustrated on pp. 147 and 148). Φ's approach to the obverse head is very much in the South Italian tradition of full if not fleshy heads which in this case perpetuates something of the general type of facial features of the mid-century. To this he adds delicate details such as the palmettes on the hair band emerging from the rolled locks of the Nymph. The style associated with the mark Γ or Π which appears on both obverse and reverse dies is more difficult to accept as the work of a single master. The first group of the three distinguished by Regling among coins so marked is already more varied than Φ's coins, but it fails to attain the balance of the other master (illustrated on pp. 146 and 151). It comprises both somewhat fleshy heads and others with thin and linear features. The second phase is related to the work of Phrygillos at Syracuse (illustrated on p. 162) and reproduces the format of that master's heads at a smaller scale, while in his last period *Pi* (Π) or *Gamma* (Γ) (depending on how one should read his marks) gives us once more heads of a decidedly heavy cast (illustrated on p. 152).

The last master to appear in the Terinian series is an unexpected figure. Late in the coinage Regling recognized the influence of Kimon, the master in whose work the Syracusan series culminated at the end of the fifth century, but it fell to Evans to read the letters of an engraver's signature on one of these dies. The name was not Kimon but Euai(netos), Kimon's great contemporary at Syracuse, who thus takes his place as the last master in the Terinian series (a similar die is illustrated on pp. 154-155)[1].

The universal appeal of the Terina series is in the reverse dies. Our selection begins with an early die made shortly after the middle of the fifth century which reproduces the reigning concept of the draped female form of the late 'Severe Style' (illustrated on p. 145 above). She is the counterpart in coinage of the graceful mirror stands of Southern Italy. The Victory seated precariously on the overturned hydria (water jar) (illustrated on p. 145 below) is drawn by a hand that thas been influenced by the crinkly drapery of the pedimental figures of the Parthenon or their counterparts in painting.

The Victory combined with the first die given to Φ shows a knowledge of the reverses of the contemporary coinage struck for the Olympia Festival in Greece (illustrated on p. 147 above) or of a common prototype. One of the reverses accompanying Φ's second obverse die is one of the most elaborate spatial compositions known in Greek coinage (illustrated on p. 147 below). The wall of the fountain house provides a background before which there are two planes made by the swan (not visible in the example illustrated here) in the middle ground and the foreshortened seat of the Victory in the foreground. The relaxed attitude of the Victory of the following illustration, shown resting against a column, has elements belonging to the most innovative Greek art of the day (illustrated on p. 148). The same pose occurs on an ancient plaster impression of a helmet cheekpiece relief now preserved in Bonn. Here, it is Aphrodite who leans against the pillar accompanied by her son Eros (illustrated on p. 148). The motive of the slipping garment also appears here, and this gesture toward nudity is known in the frequently reproduced statuary type derived from an original of the Phidian circle called the Aphrodite of Fréjus (illustrated on p. 149) and in the Victory done probably in the 420's at Olympia by Paionios, another member of the Phidian group. The relation of our Victories to such sculptural work and to the reliefs of the balustrade of the Temple of Athene Victory on the Athenian Acropolis, which are generally dated around 420, is no more than that of contemporary art drawing on similar sources. Comparisons of the seated Athene of the balustrade (illustrated on p. 153) and the coins amply illustrate this point.

[1] The reading was rejected by J. LIEGLE, *Euainetos*, 101 Winckelmannsprogramm der Archäologischen Gesellschaft zu Berlin, 1941, p. 53 note 104. However, recent study of the Syracusan series by G. K. JENKINS, 'Dionysios I of Syracuse and his Coinage', *Institute of Classical Studies, London University, Bulletin*, vol. 8, 1961, p. 86, suggests that the activity of both Kimon and Euainetos continued into the fourth century and thus supports the acceptance of the Terina inscription as an authentic signature of Euainetos.

However, Euainetos' group of Terina reverses is very different (illustrated on p. 155). These small dies have a height of relief that is remarkable even in Greek coinage and a sculptural quality that is paralleled only in raised metal work[2].

It is interesting to note that several of the Terina Victories, as well as obverse nymph heads, wear their hair gathered in a knot toward the crown of the head. This is a fashion popular for representations of Victory, and noteworthy among them is the bronze head from the Athenian Agora, which was originally plated in gold and thus may be considered a survivor of the golden Victories which were housed in the Parthenon (illustrated on p. 150).

The goddess of victory was a potent and happy artistic figure in ancient art. She evoked statues of the rank of Paionios' Victory at Olympia and the Victory of Samothrace in the Louvre. And the coins of Terina have every right to be placed beside these larger and more renowned sisters.

[2] A gold head band with a medaillon which reproduces the seated Victories of Γ is published by M. DE BRY, 'Le diadème de Terina', *Revue Archéologique*, 1971, pp. 295-298; see also E. POZZI, 'Anelli aurei italioti e tipi monetali di Terina', *Klearchos*, vol. 8, 1966, pp. 153-158.

The Velians, who reached their destination in the west from Asia Minor only in 530 B.C., fleeing Persian domination, show closer ties than the majority of the South Italian Greeks with their homeland. The regal lion, which appeared on the royal coins of the powerful Asiatic kingdom of Lydia in the middle of the sixth century and was adopted by other Greek cities of Asia Minor, Miletos, Cnidos and Samos among them, is the constant type of the new Ionian Greek city in the west as it was of Massilia (Marseilles) which had the same mother city, Phocaia (illustrated on p. 156). The obverse type of our second coin, dating from the first half of the fifth century, displays a style of execution which is also novel in the material we have been examining (illustrated on p. 156). This goddess has kept the inclined almond eyes that characterize Ionian graphic art. And her hair, done in a series of pearl-like pellets, continues the decorative preferences of Ionian taste. In view of the following obverse types of the coinage, as well as the presence of the owl on the reverse, we may be justified in calling this head Athene[1].

The crouching lion of the reverse has the stance favored for grave monuments in archaic and especially classical times. The most famous example from Italian soil is a hybrid lion, but a leonine creature none the less, the magnificent bronze Chimera from Arezzo (illustrated on p. 157). Closer to the origins of the Velian coin type, however, may be representations such as those that inspired the crouching lions on the situla from Spina by the anonymous Attic vase-painter known as the Berlin painter (illustrated on p. 158).

Our third Velian piece of about 400 has a helmeted Athene, drawn from the Attic repertoire initiated by the coins of Thurii (illustrated on p. 159). The face has lost any residual Ionianisms because of Greek mainland, and especially Attic, influences of the mid-fifth century. The reverse of this coin is an arresting scene of a lion pouncing on a deer which expands on the theme of the ravening lion already present in the city's earliest issues. The scene is known on gems from both Italy and Asia Minor, and as a coin type it was employed in the mid-fifth century by the ruler of Citium in Cyprus and then a century later by Mazaeus, the Persian ruler of Cilicia in southern Asia Minor and Adramelek, ruler of Byblos. The adoption of the type at Velia was probably motivated more by the search to extend the lion imagery of the coin than for overt reference to Cyprus and the east. However, the type was also particularly suited to Velian iconography of the lion ravening a stag's head. This motive, which recalls the eagle and stag's head of Croton, may have some Italian significance which cannot be traced further.

The facing Athene head by Kleudoros is a die of originality (illustrated on p. 160). It looks for inspira-

---

[1] On the background of the coinage see E. Pozzi, 'Problemi della monetazione di Velia', *La Parola del Passato*, vol. 130-133, 1970, pp. 166-197.

tion to the facing head dies of Catane and Syracuse (where Eukleides did his facing Athene) as well as the heads of Croton and Pandosia. But the design has been carried out so that the helmet, though still three-crested, no longer dominates the composition. The hair owes much to the Hera heads of Croton. But the result is an original and pleasing innovation.

The reverse of this coin might seem to be the prototype for the glowering lion reverse of the next Velia piece illustrated here (on p. 161). Again the obverse is signed, by Philistion, on the crest of Athene's helmet, and the Φ of the reverse possibly repeats his signature. In any case, this coin of the late fourth century is sufficient to undermine many of the attributions of South Italian coins bearing a Φ made by Charles Seltman to the Syracusan diecutter Phrygillos, who was active before 400[2].

Philistion's Athene is based on the head of the goddess as she appeared on the coins of Corinth. But the four-horse chariot on the bowl of the helmet and the single rider on the neckpiece are added ornaments that are shared with the Leukippos issues of Metapontum. Philistion's reverse is a memorable invention. The classical Greek lion, created by artists who never saw the beast in their homeland, became a kind of mastiff with leonine features, but never was this artificial animal given greater expressiveness than in this coin[3]. What is the occasion? One's thoughts turn towards a victorious battle fought along the coast in the neighborhood, but historical records fail to match intuition.

[2] C. SELTMAN, *Masterpieces of Greek Coinage*, Oxford, 1949.

[3] Other examples of the lion with a spear clutched in his jaws are found on an Etruscan urn at Volterra, *Enciclopedia dell'Arte Antica*, supp., 1971, fig. 737, and on the coins in Italy of Capua, Venusia, Mateola, Velzna, the Roman Campanian series and Aes Grave; in Greece on the Macedonian regal issues of Amyntas III and Perdiccas III and also at Pantecapaeum and Cardia. The type is also reproduced on gems. For references *cf.* W. L. BROWN, *The Etruscan Lion*, Oxford, 1960, p. 151.

ARTISTS' SIGNATURES ON SOUTH ITALIAN COINS

The status of Greek coins as works of art from a period in which the achievements of the principal masters of painting and sculpture are irretrievably lost makes the appearance of artists' signatures on them doubly interesting and important. The earliest signatures appear in the 430's at Catane (κ), Rhegium (κε) and doubtfully, in my opinion, at Acragas (EXAKESIOS)[1].

The first important concentration of engravers' names occurs on the coins of Syracuse over a span of two decades beginning in the teens of the fifth century. To this group of masters there belong the famous names of Euainetos, Kimon, Eukleides and Phrygillos, while at neighboring Catane Herakleides achieved what is possibly the most lavish effect known to a Greek coin with his facing Apollo. This coin, together with Eukleides' facing Athene and Kimon's facing Arethusa at Syracuse, set the fashion for frontal images seen at Croton, Pandosia, Metapontum and Velia.

The greatest engravers need not sign their coin dies to be identified. Innovative conception and exceptional standard of execution permit the watchful student of coin art to pick out the work of a truly outstanding master. In this way the Damareteion Master and Aitna Master have emerged from the anonymous throng of early Sicilian die cutters, and more recently, a group of engravers active in the early Syracusan series has been added to their number[2]. The attentive discussion of the coins of any mint will elicit similar distinctions of sequences of coins bound together by stylistic currents, moments of productive innovation, and, on the other hand, periods of relative stability and repetitiveness. In Magna Graecia only Rhegium, Terina, Caulonia and in part Metapontum, Heraclea and Thurii have been studied in this way[3]. Sir Arthur Evans' work on Tarentum attempted to characterize the artistic character of the successive phases of the Tarentine coinage without assembling a corpus or attempting a die study[4].

It is important to keep the state of numismatic scholarship in mind because judgments concerning authorship of dies can generally be controlled only by reference to their place in a fully established mint sequence. Some names, written out in full but in minuscule letters inconspicuously placed on the die, unquestionably identify artistic authorship[5]. Such signatures, like that of Molossos at Thurii or Ari-

---

[1] The last proposed by M. THOMPSON in *American Numismatic Society, Museum Notes*, vol. 12, 1966, pp. 6-7, a magistrate?

[2] R. R. HOLLOWAY, 'Damarete's Lion', *American Numismatic Society, Museum Notes*, vol. 11, 1964, pp. 1-11. H. SCHARMER, 'Die Meister der spätarchaischen Aretusaköpfe', *Antike Kunst*, vol. 10, 1967, pp. 94-100.

[3] Note Herzfelder's identification of artistic groups in *Les monnaies d'argent de Rhégion*.

[4] EVANS, 'The "Horsemen" of Tarentum'.

[5] An exhaustive catalogue of engravers' signatures was made by L. FORRER, 'Les signatures de graveurs sur les monnaies grecques' published serially in *Revue belge de numismatique*, vols. 59-62, 1903-1906. Forrer did not have the advantage of Regling's *Terina* or Evans' latest contribution 'Engravers of Terina and the Signature of Euainetos', *NC*, ser. 4, vol. 12, 1912,

stoxenos at Metapontum, are in the minority and generally do not seem to mark decisive moments in the history of the coinages. Marks often identified as signatures in the South Italian coinages are more often abbreviations, such as KAΛ at Tarentum, or single letters, such as Φ at Terina. When such marks have the inconspicuous character of the full length signatures, they may be accepted as artists' marks, but when they are larger and more prominently placed, it becomes difficult to distinguish them from the marks of magistrates in charge of coinage or contracting smiths responsible for its production. Indeed, Sir Arthur Evans, whose study of Tarentum remains the most detailed treatment of this subject, was forced to classify a number of these marks as engravers *signing as mint masters*, thus revealing an inability to find a clear division between the abbreviated signatures of different dimensions and stylistic judgments which seemed to unite the more official-appearing markings. It is necessary, therefore, to exercise considerable restraint in dealing with the question of artistic personalities in the coinage of Magna Graecia. It is not only the absence of full mint studies, but the plethora of eligible marks (30 separate letters at Velia in the British Museum, *Catalogue of Greek Coins, Italy*, for example) that complicate the situation.

We must count on the activity of one of the Syracusan masters in Italy, the greatest of them, Euainetos. Late in the Terina series in the early fourth century the familiar signature EYAI appears on the hair band of the seated Nike of the Terina reverse joined with an obverse recalling the Persephone of Euainetos' Syracusan decadrachms. Since this Euainetean head was widely imitated in Greek coinage of the fourth century, its occurence at Terina alone would not suffice to show that Euainetos worked for the mint, but the signature is unequivocal and the coins fully worthy of the great Syracusan master.

At the time when the Syracusan masters began to sign their dies, an artist on the mainland adds a modest Φ to his dies, generally behind the neck of the head of the obverse side. His work can be defined best at Terina, thanks to the die study of this coinage made in 1906 by Kurt Regling[6]. The appearance of Φ's signature (with Γ, an associate?) comes at a decisive moment in the Terinian series when the obverse heads lose the slightly provincial character they have had earlier and acquire a distinctly Syracusan cast, while the Victories of the reverses become pictorially conceived figures surrounded by their oustretched wings[7].

pp. 21-62. L. TUDEER's 'Die Tetradrachmenprägung von Syrakus in der Periode der signierenden Künstler', *Zeitschrift für Numismatik*, vol. 30, 1913, pp. 1-292 was also in the future when Forrer wrote. For the last fifty years the signatures in South Italy have received rather little attention, if one excepts C. SELTMAN's *Masterpieces of Greek Coinage*, Oxford, 1949, and J. H. JONGKEES' *The Kimonian Dekadrachm*, Leiden, 1941, pp. 74-78.

[6] Regling, *Terina*.
[7] ADOLF FÜRTWANGLER, *Meisterwerke griechischer Kunst*, English Tr. Sellers, London, 1895, pp. 105-107, following R.

Φ is also found in contemporary issues of Thurii, both staters and distaters, in the field by the head of Athene, much in the same manner as it accompanies the obverse images at Terina. Stylistically, these heads have much in common, and in particular a furrow extending downward from the inner corner of the lips, a repeated mannerism suggesting common authorship. In both cases, the heads have a similar reduced size in respect to the flan when compared to earlier parts of the series. It is less certain that the letters Φ or ΦΡΥ on the reverse of the Thurian issues are also the signature of the artist. A further extension of his name would identify him with the small bird also found below the Thurian bulls and originally identified by A. Sambon as a finch, in Greek 'Phrygilos'[8]. This identification would make the Φ of Terina and Thurii the same artist, who signed one die and made others in the Syracusan tetradrachm series as well. This engraver may also be identical with Phrygillos the gem cutter of the fifth century whose signed work is represented by a gem (representing an Eros) now in Berlin. Unfortunately for the reconstruction of a versatile and far-ranging artistic career however, the style of the Syracusan master, which displays a strongly personal touch in heads that seem to accent the area of the eye through a heavy and rather old-fashioned eyebrow while at the same time moving the features of the face somewhat toward the front of the profile head, does not correspond at all to the formal balance of the representations at Terina and Thurii (illustrated on p. 162). The turn of the mouth that we noted earlier as characteristic of Φ's work is also noticeably lacking in Phrygillos' coins.

It is less easy to put aside Φ's claim to the splendid Pandosia series with facing goddess and seated Pan for the reverse type. There is a Φ in the reverse field. But the letter is a little too prominent for an artist's signature, while on the British Museum specimen the inscription ΦΑΛΛΟΝ was read by Evans on the herm facing the seated Pan[9]. The dimensions are more appropriate to an artist's signature, and the ithyphallic herm is possibly a punning conceit on the artist's name. Other attributions to Phrygillos at Leontini and at Sinope on the Black Sea coast seem to have, at best, an element of fancy about them[10].

More consideration is due to questions raised by the appearance of the letter Φ on coins of Heraclea and Tarentum. The importance of artistic developments in the coinage of Tarentum connected with the

STUART-POOLE, 'Athenian Coin-engravers in Italy', NC, 3rd ser., vol. 3, 1883, pp. 269-277 stressed the relation of Φ and his contemporaries to the art of Athens in the Phidian and post-Phidian era. I would prefer to regard Athens, which was unquestionably the most important artistic center in Greece of this time, as the eventual source of inspiration rather than necessarily the immediate training ground of the South Italian engravers.

[8] *Cat. Maddalena*, 1903, p. 409.

[9] *NC*, 4th ser., vol. 12, 1912, p. 30.

[10] SELTMAN, *Masterpieces of Greek Coinage*, pp. 66-81, JONGKEES, *The Kimonian Dekadrachm*, pp. 74-78, accepts a common authorship of Phrygillos and Φ at Syracuse, Terina, Thurii, Pandosia, Velia, and Heraclea.

appearance of Φ and associated designations, especially A and κ, was emphasized in the fundamental study of Sir Arthur Evans[11]. In brief, the engravers active at the time when these identifications (which Evans believed were engravers' signatures) were introduced in the first half of the fourth century liberated Tarentine coinage from the formulas which had satisfied the preceding century. Instead, they gave the dolphin rider Phalanthos a turning posture, introduced similar graphic elements throughout the coinage, and brought the boy jockey to the series. Evans found the source of the torsion-filled figures of these engravers in the type of standing Heracles wrestling with the Nemean lion at Heraclea. The type was established early in the history of the Heraclean mint (which could have come into being on the foundation of the city in 432). But after a lapse of some years, possibly in the early fourth century, the letter Φ (as well as EY and Σ) appears in the field. Although Evans' judgment of the artistic current bringing designs with advanced contrapposto into South Italian coin art is worthy of respect, his search for artists' signatures was possibly too enthusiastic. In the series at Heraclea there are two definite signatures, ARISTOXENOS in minute letters along the base of Athene's crest on one die and EUPHRO on the exergue line of a reverse. These signatures are similar to ISTOROS, MOLOSSOS, and NIKANDROS at Thurii, and KLEUDOROS and PHILISTION at Velia and KRATESIPPOS at Rhegium. The letters in the field are, in my opinion, official control marks.

The preceding remarks should in no way reflect on Evan's brilliant perception of the development of the Tarentine series. Without the benefit of a complete mint study he was able to group the coins by their stylistic relationships and sketch with great conviction the artistic trends of the fourth century which weave their way through the coinage. The progressive and spatially conceived development which he found associated with coins marked Φ, KAΛ, and A do not mean, however, that these marks are signatures. Evans himself on occasion found refuge in the assumption that they designated engravers signing as minting officials. And one can appreciate his insights into the artistic trends of the series without accepting his contention that these letter marks stand for artists' names.

One or more of these same control marks appearing on coins of Neapolis, Heraclea and Metapontum is hardly enough evidence to prove reference to the same name, to say nothing of proving that reference to the same person is intended. But the occurrences at the last two mints of letter designations also known at Tarentum call for further discussion because of their geographical proximity and other stylistic considerations.

At Metapontum we meet the artist ARISTOXENOS who signs in full in minuscule letters on the reverse of a single, but elegant issue with an obverse head of Persephone. The cautious numismatist

[11] EVANS, 'The ''Horsemen'' of Tarentum'.

Sydney P. Noe was prepared to accept the bold letter A's on the obverses of this same Metapontine group as abbreviations of ARISTOXENOS and furthermore to identify him with A at Heraclea[12]. He further compared A's wrestling Heracles with the seated Apollo of Metapontum discussed earlier and assigned them to a common artist. This analysis does not accord with our discussion here nor with the derivation of the Apollo type from a source in painting proposed earlier.

For Evans and Forrer the connection between the Tarentine and Metapontine mints also lay in coins marked A, ΑΠΟΛ at Metapontum, which they considered an artist's signature. This association is especially marked in the veiled head found in Tarentine gold and Metapontine silver issues (illustrated on p. 163). These Tarentine coins, like all gold of independent cities (as contrasted with that of the Macedonian and Hellenistic monarchies), must have been emergency issues, and both issues seem to belong to the years of urgency culminating in the expedition of Alexander the Molossian to Italy and momentary Italiote Greek union under his banner in the late 330's. The identity of concept of the coins, therefore, may be due as much to political circumstances as to artistic initiative independent of the cities' policies. The same holds for the connections between coins maked ΚΑΛ at Tarentum (notably the supplication gold) and Metapontine issues.

In Southern Italy, therefore, we find evidence of a number of artists who signed single issues with their full name and one by abbreviation, Φ. He is the earliest and the most important, having worked at Terina and Thurii. Otherwise, the authorship of the die engravings must be extracted from the series of coins and this task, in most cases, awaits completion of mint studies[13].

[12] *The Coinage of Metapontum* (Part Two), Numismatic Notes and Monographs, 47, New York, 1931, pp. 30-41. This and others of Evans' identifications were criticized by S. W. GROSE from the point of view of the coinage of Heraclea in 'Primitiae Heraclienses', *NC*, 4th ser., vol. 17, 1917, pp. 169-189.

[13] In a most interesting dissertation entitled *Matrici di figure fittili femminili del IV-III sec. a.C. da Eraclea di Lucania*, presented at the State University of Milan in 1976, Dr. Giovanna Ceccatelli has pointed out cases of makers' marks identical to coin 'signatures' on terracotta molds, thus raising the possibility of the wider consideration of this question with regard to the general organization of industrial production at Heraclea and at Tarentum in the fourth and third centuries. For the general question of the relationship between coin types, especially of Thurii and Heraclea, and surviving gems see G. M. A. RICHTER, *Engraved Gems of the Greeks and the Etruscans*, London, 1968, pp. 23-25.

The photographs of coins in this volume are principally by Carpi, Bellinzona, with the exception of the photographs on pp. 75, 76, 77 by Ventura, Milan, on pp. 75, 89, 90, 91, 102, 147, 163 by Hirmer Verlag, Munich and on pp. 154, 155 by American Numismatic Society, New York. Further photographs have been provided by Alinari, Florence (pp. 141, 157), Allard Pierson Museum, Amsterdam (p. 114), American School of Classical Studies, Agora Excavations, Athens (pp. 138, 150), Antiken Museum, Basel (pp. 92, 93), Brown University, Archaeological Expedition (p. 113), British Museum, London (p. 109), Cleveland Museum of Art (p. 129), Deutsches Archäologisches Institut, Rom (p. 103), Fogg Art Museum, Howard University (p. 143), Hirmer Verlag, Munich (pp. 78, 79, 80, 81, 82, 83, 88, 94, 99, 105, 107, 119, 121, 137, 140, 153, 158), Musée du Louvre, Paris (p. 149), Museum of Fine Arts, Boston (p. 95), National Archaeological Museum, Reggio Calabria (p. 144), Provincial Archaeological Museum, Salerno (p. 133), Staatliche Museen, Berlin (pp. 86, 87, 123), Universitätsmuseum, Bonn (photo Peter Pruy, p. 148).

Plates

Tarentum. Stater. 520-510 B.C.

Caulonia. Stater. 530-510 B.C.

Poseidonia. Stater. 540–510 B.C.

Croton. Stater. 550–530 B.C.

Metapontum. Stater. 530–510 B.C.

Sybaris. Stater. 530–510 B.C.

Frieze of the Siphnian Treasury at Delphi. Battle of Gods and Giants. Marble. Delphi Museum. ca. 525 B.C.

Metope of the Temple of Zeus at Olympia.
Heracles presenting the Stymphalian Birds to Athene. Marble. Louvre. 460 B.C.

Ionic Frieze of the Parthenon, Athens. Restored Archaic Dedications of the Acropolis. Marble. Louvre. 440 B.C.

Parapet surrounding the precinct of Athene Victory, Athens, Acropolis. A Victory. Marble. Acropolis Museum. ca. 420 B.C.

Bronze God, Zeus or Poseidon. Athens, National Museum. ca. 460 B.C.

Charioteer from bronze group of a four-horse chariot dedicated by Polyzalos of Gela at Delphi. Delphi Museum. ca. 475 B.C.

Croton. Stater. 410-350 B.C.

84

Ceiling painting from the Tomb of the Diver, Poseidonia. Paestum Museum. ca. 485 B.C.

Seated Goddess from Tarentum. Marble. Berlin, Staatliche Museen. ca. 480 B.C.

Seated Goddess from Tarentum. Marble. Berlin, Staatliche Museen. ca. 480 B.C.

Red-figured amphora attributed to the Carneiades Painter. Dionysos and followers. Taranto, National Museum. ca. 410 B.C.

*Bronze toilet-box (cista) from Praeneste, the
'Ficoroni Cista' (detail, drawing of design).
Rome, Villa Giulia Museum.   ca. 350 B.C.*

Tarentum.   Gold Stater.   344-334 B.C.

Tarentum. Stater. ca. 480 B.C.

Aitna. Tetradrachm. ca. 476 B.C.

Red-figured amphora attributed to the Berlin Painter. Heracles. Basel, Antikenmuseum. ca. 490 B.C.

92

Red-figured amphora attributed to the Berlin Painter. Athene. Basel, Antikenmuseum. ca. 490 B.C.

Disc with female head from Melos. Marble. Athens, National Museum. ca 450 B.C.

Tarentum. Stater. 480-470 B.C.

Bronze head of youth. Boston, Museum of Fine Arts, Catharine Page Perkins Fund. ca. 520 B.C.

Tarentum. Stater. 470-460 B.C.

Tarentum. Stater. 450-430 B.C.

Tarentum. Stater. 420–380 B.C.

Tarentum. Stater. 380–345 B.C.

97

Tarentum. Stater. 344-334 B.C.

The 'Stele from the Ilissos', marble grave relief with scene of mourning. Athens, National Museum. ca. 330 B.C.

Tarentum. Stater. 334-330 B.C.

Tarentum. Stater. 302–281 B.C.

Tarentum. Gold Stater. 334-330 B.C.

Head of Zeus, from Cyrene. Cyrene Museum. Ancient marble replica of original of the later fifth century B.C.

Rhegium. Tetradrachm. 445-435 B.C.

Rhegium. Tetradrachm. 435-425 B.C.

Ionic Frieze of the Parthenon, Athens. Poseidon, Apollo, Artemis. Marble. Acropolis Museum. 440 B.C.

Rhegium. Tetradrachm. 488–480 B.C.

Zankle-Messina. Tetradrachm. 493–488 B.C.

Frieze of the Siphnian Treasury at Delphi. Battle of Gods and Giants, detail. Marble. Delphi Museum. ca. 525 B.C.

Messina. Tetradrachm. 488–480 B.C.

Bronze model shield (lacunarium) from Tarquinia. London, British Museum. Late sixth century B.C.

Rhegium. Tetradrachm. 480-461 B.C.

Rhegium. Tetradrachm. 415/410-387 B.C.

Catane. Tetradrachm. ca. 420 B.C.

Catane. Tetradrachm. ca. 410 B.C.

Impression from terracotta mold. Silenus. Padula, Archaeological Museum of Western Lucania.
Prototype of mold late fifth century B.C.

Fragment of a red-figured crater. Apollo before his temple. Amsterdam, Allard Pierson Museum. ca. 350 B.C.

Rhegium. Tetradrachm. 356-351 B.C.

Poseidonia. Stater. 440–420 B.C.

Poseidonia. Stater. 350–325 B.C.

116

Caulonia. Stater. 435-425 B.C.

Metapontum. Stater. 490–450 B.C.

Metapontum. Stater. 485–440 B.C.

Red-figured crater attributed to the Niobid Painter. A group of gods and heroes. Louvre. ca. 440 B.C.

Metapontum. Stater. 485-440 B.C.

The 'Apollo of the Omphalos'. Athens, National Museum.
Ancient marble replica of original of about 460 B.C.

Metapontum. Stater. 450–400 B.C.

Red-figured crater attributed to the Orpheus Painter. Orpheus performing for a group of Thracians. Berlin, Staatliche Museen. ca. 440 B.C.

Metapontum. Stater. 435-350 B.C.

Metapontum. Stater. 435-350 B.C.

Metapontum. Stater. 330–300 B.C.

Metapontum. Stater. 400–360 B.C.

126

Metapontum. Distater. 330-300 B.C.

Thurii. Stater. 443–400 B.C.

Thurii. Stater. 415–375 B.C.

Bronze figurine of a bull. Cleveland Museum of Art, purchase from the J.H. Wade Fund. Fifth century B.C. (?).

Heraclea. Stater. ca. 432 B.C.

Heraclea. Stater. 410–400 B.C.

Heraclea. Stater. 433–330 B.C.

Heraclea. Stater. 433–375 B.C.

132

Syracuse. 100 litrae gold. ca. 390 B.C.

Terracotta antefix. Heracles and the Nemean lion.
Salerno, Provincial Archaeological Museum.
Fourth century B.C. (?).

Heraclea-Stater. 433–330 B.C.

Heraclea-Stater. 433–375 B.C.

Heraclea. Stater. ca. 280 B.C.

Alexander the Great. Gold stater. After 336 B.C.

Croton. Stater. 420-390 B.C.

Croton. Stater. 420-390 B.C.

136

Red-figured crater attributed to the Cleophon Painter, from Spina. Procession to Apollo at Delphi. Ferrara, National Museum. ca. 430 B.C.

*Ancient plaster cast of a buckle from the
Athenian Agora. Odysseus (?) resting.
Athens, Agora Museum. ca. 400 B.C.*

Croton. Stater. 420–390 B.C.

Croton. Stater. 410-350 B.C.

Seated male god or hero 'Theseus'. Parthenon East Pediment. Marble. London, British Museum. 440 B.C.

Croton. Stater. 400–350 B.C.

Bronze helmet cheek-piece from Praeneste. Heracles.
Rome, Villa Giulia Museum. Fourth century B.C.

Pandosia. Stater. ca. 400 B.C.

Bronze helmet cheek-piece. Hunter and dog.
Fogg Art Museum, Harvard University, Frederick R. Grace Memorial. Fourth century B.C.

Pandosia. Bronze unit. ca. 400 B.C.

Terracotta plaque. Subject uncertain.
From Medma. Reggio Calabria, National Museum.
Late fifth century B.C. (?)

Terina. Stater. 480–450 B.C.

Terina. Stater. 445–425 B.C.

Terina. Stater. 425–420 B.C.

Elis. Stater. 430–420 B.C.

Terina. Stater. 425–420 B.C.

147

Terina. Stater. 420-400 B.C.

Ancient plaster cast of a helmet cheek-piece. Aphrodite and Eros.
Bonn, Universitätsmuseum. ca. 420 B.C.

The 'Aphrodite of Fréjus'. Louvre.
Ancient marble replica of original of the later fifth century B.C.

Bronze head of a goddess (Victory?) from the Athenian Agora. Athens, Agora Museum. ca. 430 B.C.

Terina. Stater. 420–400 B.C.

Terina. Stater. 420–400 B.C.

Marble parapet surrounding the precinct of Athene Victory, Athens, Acropolis. Athens. Acropolis Museum. ca. 420 B.C.

Terina. Stater. after 400 B.C.

Velia. Drachm. 530-490 B.C.

Velia. Stater. before 450 B.C.

156

The 'Arezzo Chimera', bronze. Florence, Archaeological Museum. Fourth century B.C. (?).

Red-figured situla attributed to the Berlin Painter. Detail, a lion. Ferrara, National Museum. ca. 490 B.C.

Velia. Stater. 420–380 B.C.

Velia. Stater. 380-340 B.C.

Velia. Stater. after 320 B.C.

Syracuse. Tetradrachm. ca. 412 B.C.

Tarentum. Gold Stater. 344-334 B.C.

Metapontum. Stater. 344-334 B.C.

BIBLIOGRAPHY

Principal historical works dealing with the fifth and fourth centuries B.C.

E. CIACERI, *Storia della Magna Grecia*, 3 vol., Milan, 1927-1932.
G. GIANNELLI, *La Magna Grecia da Pitagora a Pirro*, Milan, 1928.
F. LENORMANT, *La Grande Grèce*, 2nd ed., 3 vol., Paris, 1881-1884.
E. PAIS, *Storia della Sicilia e Magna Grecia*, vol. I, Palermo, 1894.

General works with extensive bibliography

J. BÉRARD, *Bibliographie topographique des principales cités grecques de l'Italie méridionale et de la Sicilie dans l'antiquité*, Paris, 1941.
L. BREGLIA, *Arte e Moneta, I, Magna Grecia*, Naples, 1959.
G. GIANNELLI, *Culti e Miti della Magna Grecia*, ed. 2, Milan, 1963.
D. MUSTILLI, 'Civiltà della Magna Grecia', in *Metropoli e Colonie di Magna Grecia, Atti del Terzo Convegno di Studi sulla Magna Grecia*, 1964, pp. 5-47.
M. NAPOLI, *Civiltà della Magna Grecia*, Rome, 1969.
A. G. WOODHEAD, *The Greeks in the West*, London, 1962.

ABBREVIATIONS

Cahn	H. A. CAHN, 'Early Tarentine Chronology', *Essays in Greek Coinage presented to Stanley Robinson*, Oxford, 1968.
Evans	J. A. EVANS, 'The "Horsemen" of Tarentum', *Numismatic Chronicle*, ser. 3, vol. 9, 1889.
Franke	P. R. FRANKE, M. HIRMER, *Die Griechische Münze*, ed. 2, Munich, 1972.
Head	B. V. HEAD, *Historia Numorum*, ed. 2, Oxford, 1911.
Herzfelder	H. HERZFELDER, *Les monnaies d'argent de Rhégion*, Paris, 1957.
Jenkins	G.K. JENKINS, *Ancient Greek Coins*, London, New York, Toronto, 1972.
Kraay	C. KRAAY, *Greek Coins* (English edition of Franke and Hirmer, *Die Griechische Münze*), London, 1966.
Naster	P. NASTER, *La collection Lucien de Hirsch*, Brussels, 1959.
NC	*Numismatic Chronicle*
Noe	S. P. NOE, *The Coinage of Metapontum* (Part Two), Numismatic Notes and Monographs no. 47, New York, 1931.
Regling	K. REGLING, *Terina*, 66 Programm zum Winckelmannsfeste, Berlin, 1906.
Robinson	E. S. G. ROBINSON, *A Catalogue of the Calouste Gulbenkian Collection of Greek Coins*, Part 1, Lisbon, 1971.
Work	E. WORK, *The Earlier Staters of Heracleia Lucaniae*, Numismatic Notes and Monographs no. 91, New York, 1940.

CONTENTS

Finito di stampare
il sette marzo millenovecentosettantotto
nell'officina dell'Istituto grafico Casagrande SA
Bellinzona (Svizzera)